Not by Politics Alone ...
– The Other Lenin

This title is one of a series published to commemorate the centenary of V. I. Lenin's death. The others are as follows:

Imperialism and the National Question, V. I. Lenin
The State and Revolution, V. I. Lenin

Lenin's Childhood, Isaac Deutscher

Not by Politics Alone ...
– The Other Lenin

edited and introduced by
Tamara Deutscher

VERSO
London • New York

This edition first published by Verso 2024
First published by George Allen & Unwin Ltd 1973
© Verso 2024

1 3 5 7 9 10 8 6 4 2

Verso
UK: 6 Meard Street, London W1F 0EG
US: 388 Atlantic Avenue, Brooklyn, NY 11217
versobooks.com

Verso is the imprint of New Left Books

ISBN-13: 978-1-80429-274-7
ISBN-13: 978-1-80429-275-4 (UK EBK)
ISBN-13: 978-1-80429-276-1 (US EBK)

British Library Cataloguing in Publication Data
A catalogue record for this book is available from the British Library

Library of Congress Cataloging-in-Publication Data

Names: Lenin, Vladimir Il'ich, 1870-1924, author. | Deutscher, Tamara,
    editor. | Lenin, Vladimir Il'ich, 1870-1924. Works. Selections. English
Title: Not by politics alone : the other Lenin / V.I. Lenin ; edited and
    introduced by Tamara Deutscher.
Description: [First Verso edition.] | Brooklyn, NY : Verso, 2024. | "First
    published by George Allen & Unwin Ltd 1973"—Copyright page. | Includes
    bibliographical references and index.
Identifiers: LCCN 2023036229 (print) | LCCN 2023036230 (ebook) | ISBN
    9781804292747 (trade paperback) | ISBN 9781804292761 (US ebk)
Subjects: LCSH: Lenin, Vladimir Il'ich, 1870-1924.
Classification: LCC DK254.L4 D48 2024 (print) LCC DK254.L4 (ebook) |
    DDC 947.084/1092 [B]—dc23/eng/20230822
LC record available at https://lccn.loc.gov/2023036229
LC ebook record available at https://lccn.loc.gov/2023036230

Printed and bound by CPI Group (UK) Ltd, Croydon CR0 4YY

PREFACE

A choice of excerpts for an anthology is always somewhat arbitrary. Much more – reminiscences, letters and quotations – might have been included here in order to show that Lenin did not live by politics alone. Quite deliberately I have kept out of this volume such writers as Krupskaya, Trotsky or Gorky, because each of their books on Lenin constitutes an entity from which it would be wrong to cull short passages. Their works are easily available; they are lively, extremely readable and informative. If a somewhat different Lenin emerges from their pens, it is because each of them was a different – and a strong – personality and this coloured their narrative. Nor have I used Lenin's letters to his relatives which form a whole volume of his *Collected Works*.

Whenever possible I have tried to go to original Russian sources less known to the Western public; also to bring in the recollections of people who had worked with Lenin for some length of time. As the reader will see from the letter to Inessa Armand reproduced on page 120, Lenin often used to underline words for emphasis. In those of his letters which appear in this book ordinary italics have been used to indicate single underlining and bold italics where Lenin vigorously underlined a word two or three times or more.

I should like to thank Lawrence and Wishart for their generous permission to quote from their edition of Lenin's *Collected Works*; in some instances, as I explain in the Introduction, I had to revert to the latest, fifth Russian edition and provide my own translation. The Oxford University Press kindly allowed me to quote from N. Valentinov, *Encounters with Lenin*; thanks are also due to *Preuves* for permission to quote Marcel Body's article, and to the University of Michigan Press for the excerpt from A. Balabanoff's *Impressions of Lenin*.

I should like to thank most warmly all my friends who were so good as to help me in my work. Professor E. F. C. Ludowyk once again showed admirable patience in scrutinising the text and my translation and in trying, with infinite tact, to smooth many of my most ungraceful turns of phrase. To Mr F. Samson

I am grateful for his most attentive reading of the typescript, for his valuable criticism and also for constant encouragement. My thanks are due to Mr Monty Johnstone, who very kindly put at my disposal his library, helped in the search for some sources and thus spared me hours of unproductive toil. The very first, and nebulous, idea of *Not by Politics Alone* . . . emerged from a talk with an American student, Steven Unger. It was his generation of readers, those born after the Second World War, that I had primarily in mind while preparing this anthology.

T.D.

CONTENTS

V WOMEN'S RIGHTS

VI BUREAUCRACY

INTRODUCTION

More than any other historical figure, Lenin determined the character and the outlook of our epoch. He developed Marx's conception of proletarian socialism and brought the fabric of his vision within the ken of the exploited and oppressed masses of the vast Tsarist empire. As a leader of men, he gave purpose and direction to social forces which, disjointed and dispersed, might have spent themselves and achieved nothing. He speeded up a historical process, gave it shape and form, and was the prime mover of events which shook the world. Yet he was no Nietzschean Superman nor a demiurge of history, but was himself shaped and formed by circumstances. His greatness consisted precisely in this: he was the perfect expression of the needs of his time; he saw farther and deeper than most men of his time, and he had an extraordinary insight into those urges and longings of which people, still shackled by an anachronistic mode of existence, had only vague and half-conscious awareness. He formulated the thoughts which agitated the rank and file of his party; he knew the meaning and weight of the clouds which drifted in the air and across the dark skies of autocratic Russia; he harnessed all the winds of change to unleash the storm in which the old established order of government was to founder. When he acted, he acted in accord with the masses. He was their undisputed leader; he was also led by them.

When on the morrow of the great October insurrection he calmly declared: 'now we shall proceed to build a new social order', in front of him were less than six years during which he exercised power. Behind him was a quarter of a century of prison, exile, clandestine work, and emigration; a quarter of a century of strenuous preparatory and educative endeavour. By 1917 Lenin, the philosopher, theoretician, economist, journalist, polemicist, literary and social critic, had already produced his great works: *The Development of Capitalism in Russia, What is to be Done?, Materialism and Empirio-Criticism.* Just before October, poised on the Finnish border and in hiding, he worked on *The State and Revolution* which he began with a prophetic remark on the attempts to convert the revolutionary thinkers, after their death, into 'harmless icons', to canonise them, while at the same time robbing their revolutionary theory of its substance. The last chapter of the treatise – on the lessons of 1905 and 1917 – was never written: the actual uprising left no time for this: '. . . it was more pleasant and useful to go through the "experience of the revolution" than to write about it', remarked Lenin a few weeks later.[1]

It is not the aim of this volume to introduce the reader to the essentials of Leninism or to summarise or pre-digest for him Lenin's monumental ideas. The other Lenin will emerge from these pages: the other and yet the same, the Lenin of everyday reality who lived by politics but not by politics alone, the Lenin of work and leisure, geared to his life's purpose and yet enjoying to the full all the pleasures of a healthy human existence; neither the humourless monolithic cult-hero of the official mythology nor the humourless bogey man of official anti-communism.

What perhaps impressed Trotsky most in Lenin's personality – he stressed this time and time again – was Lenin's singleness of purpose, his extraordinarily tense, unrelenting straining towards his goal: the overthrow of the old autocratic tsarist order and the building up of the foundations of the new, socialist one. Even a less perspicacious observer, and one for whom this tautness of purpose as well as the purpose itself were not matters for admiration, was struck by this characteristic feature: 'The idea which had taken hold of him', writes Valentinov, the future Menshevik who in his youth was under Lenin's spell, 'at any given moment to tally dominates his mind, turning him into a man possessed. It seemed as if all other aspects of his mental life, all his other interests and wishes, were swept aside and vanished during such periods. There was one idea alone, nothing else, in Lenin's field of vision: one brightly shining point in the darkness . . ..'[2] The 'one idea' was of such dimensions that it could indeed have filled completely the whole field of vision.

Lenin was not drawn into revolutionary activities on an impulse, by a society in turmoil or on the verge of an upheaval; he chose the life of a professional revolutionary deliberately, after mature reflection, and with eyes fully open. The road dimly perceived by Alexander Ulyanov, his older brother who had perished on the gallows, the road to the transformation of society through society's own awareness of its wretchedness, through the realisation of the masses of their own strength and potentialities acquired in the course of slow educative work, that road became Lenin's long before he glimpsed any hope that in his strivings for his idea, he would ever live to see its fulfilment. Yet, his whole being 'was geared to one purpose', the purpose of the revolution.

This absolute dedication of his life, this subordination of all inessentials to the needs and requirements of the ultimate aim did not, and could not, make of Lenin a wooden icon of Stalinist hagiography nor the soulless, narrow-minded 'compulsive' revolutionary portrayed by Western philistines organically incapable of comprehending the motive power of a truly great idea.

> He is earthly –
> > but not of those
> > > whose nose
> delves only into
> > their own little sty.
> He grasped the earth
> > whole,
> > > all at one go . . .

Mayakovsky said of him.[3] Precisely because Lenin's aim was so great and all-embracing, precisely because it concerned the whole of humanity, there was nothing narrow in his outlook; precisely because he acted as he did in the interest of ordinary men and women and expressed their aspiration and unspoken thoughts, it could be truly said of him that no field of human endeavour was alien to him.

Stalin needed the cult of Lenin's personality before he could embark on building up his own; the innumerable monuments he raised to Lenin were to serve him as stepping-stones or as plinths on which to raise his own statues. And yet the real Lenin was quite unlike the commanding figure in the windswept coat standing high above his native Simbirsk, with his arms out-stretched in the histrionic gesture of a Roman emperor ordering his legions to advance – as the sculptor G. Manizer depicted him. Nor did he radiate an incandescent light, a saintly halo playing around his whole body, by which this supernatural being is instantly recognised as in the paintings of a Gerasimov. If Lenin towered above the men of his time, it was by the sheer strength of his thought and by that concord of political imagination and realism which allowed him to see what was to be and did not prevent him from seeing what was. But all this could hardly be conveyed by official sculptors and official portrait painters, who had to paint Lenin in the image in which Stalin the Leader saw himself and wanted others – millions of others – to see him.

In real life Lenin's physical appearance was strikingly unremarkable (see p. 49). This ordinariness shocked the young Koba-Djugashvili – Stalin, who later recollected that preparing himself to meet Lenin for the first time he 'had hoped to see the mountain eagle of our party', the great man, great physically as well as politically. 'I had fancied Lenin as a giant, stately and imposing. How great was my disappointment to see a most ordinary-looking man, below average height, in no way, literally in no way, distinguishable from ordinary mortals. . . .' This 'most ordinary-looking man' also behaved in a most outrageously ordinary manner: 'Usually a great man comes late to a meeting so that his appearance may be awaited with bated breath. . . . How great was my disappointment to see that Lenin had arrived at the conference before the other delegates were there and had settled himself somewhere in a corner and was unassumingly carrying on a conversation, a most ordinary conversation with the most ordinary delegates.'[4]

With a less acute feeling of disappointment many of Lenin's contemporaries also commented on his unassuming manner and inconspicuous appearance. That he 'carried on an ordinary conversation' did not mean, however, that Lenin was at all capable of small or insignificant talk. For this he was too concentrated, too much 'geared to his purpose'. But he had a special way of conversing which in a casual observer only, strengthened the impression of his ordinariness. Unlike other great men, who talked at their interlocutors displaying before them their knowledge and wisdom, Lenin asked questions – and listened to the answers. Trotsky describes his first meeting with Lenin, when he burst into Lenin's flat in the very early hours of an October day in 1902 and breathlessly related to him his recent escape from Verkholensk and all the adventures encountered on the way. The same morning, or perhaps the next day, the two men went out ostensibly to look at the sights of London. But, says Trotsky, 'Vladimir Ilyich had something else in mind . . . he wanted to get to know me and to examine me.' And, indeed, during the long walk Trotsky was answering questions – all sorts of questions on the composition of the colony of deportees, on the formation of political groupings, on the various tendencies among them, on theoretical differences in the assessment of Bernstein and Kautsky, on philosophical, political and organisational quarrels, on what Trotsky's companions read and discussed in the Moscow transfer prison, and what were their comments on *The Development of Capitalism in Russia.*

This persistent questioning to which Lenin subjected anybody who managed to come abroad, whether it be a worker-delegate to a Congress, an intellectual connected with clandestine activity, or an escapee from a remote corner of the county to which he had been banished by the tsarist court, enabled him in Geneva, Zurich or London to keep in the closest possible contact with the thoughts and feelings and moods of people in Russia (see p. 58). When he finally returned to the country, in April 1917, more perhaps than any other emigré, he felt immediately at home, as if the long years in foreign parts had faded away. He was immediately at one with the masses and with the party, but also ahead of them.

Out of thirty years of political activity, he spent twenty-four as an outlaw, an underground fighter, a political prisoner, an exile. All these years this 'most earthly of all men', this great realist, was sustained by nothing more than a dream, a dream of a better, a more just, social order. 'A Bolshevik who does not dream is a bad Bolshevik', he used to say. For a quarter of a century he was working towards a goal which seemed to him even more remote than it eventually proved to be. As late as January 1917 he still did not believe that the revolution would come in the lifetime of his generation – and this was only a few months before he returned to Russia. Before the year was out, the revolution had triumphed, and he assumed power which he was to exercise for the most difficult six years of his life.

The two and a half decades he spent in exile were, for all their revolutionary fervour, marked by that considered and deliberate mode of life which one adopts facing a long, long haul, when strength cannot be treated prodigally or wasted. Many reminiscences of his fellow-emigrés testify to the well-regulated routine in which not only work, but leisure and rest had their well-defined place. He detested Bohemian revolutionism: it was incompatible with his rationality and purposefulness. But he had the gift of enjoying to the full those pleasures of life which did not interfere with his capacity for work, but on the contrary enhanced it. This showed itself even in the manner in which, as far as it was possible, he used to choose his living quarters during his constant peregrinations. Provided he had a roof over his head, a table to work at, and some shelves for his books, he was not concerned either with the aesthetic qualities of his home or with more than rudimentary comforts. What was decisive, however, was the nearness of a river so that he could skate in the winter and swim in the summer; the proximity of mountains for climbing, or even plain fields and meadows for walking and cycling. When in 1912 he came to live for a time in Cracow, he was not deterred by the dirt, mud and slums of its working-class suburb, but attracted by the Wolski forest and the *Blonie* (meadows), which so charmed Inessa Armand on one of her visits, that she took as her pseudonym, Blonina – woman of the meadows.[5] In nearby Poronin, in the foot-hills of the Tatra mountains, no less beautiful than the Alps, Lenin found that 'the view not only was not distracting, but on the contrary, helped me to concentrate'.[6]

Daily walks, swimming, skating, cycling, were part of the normal routine of life, not only because Lenin enjoyed these activities from adolescence, but also because they kept him in good physical condition, and this, he maintained, was the duty of every revolutionary. He felt it was important to adhere to the strictest physical discipline in prison, where one's morale depended on the state of one's health. It worried Lenin that his younger brother after only a few weeks in the cell had 'already begun to look puffy'; and from distant Siberian Shushenskoye he impressed on him the need to do 'physical jerks' regularly: 'he must bow not less than fifty times without bending his legs and must touch the floor with his fingers each time.'[7] Three-quarters of a century later, an apprentice revolutionary whose life was so cruelly cut short followed these recommendations with a vengeance. 'I am well, and working hard; four hours a day on exercises . . . one thousand fingertip push-ups a day', wrote George Jackson from Soledad prison reassuring his friends that though locked up without air and sun for twenty-four hours a day in isolation, he continued to train himself towards achieving 'a *delicate balance* of both mental and physical forcefulness' indispensable for a leader of a successful mass movement.

When, after 1917, the great leader of a 'successful mass movement' was already at the head of the first revolutionary government and the strains and stresses of war, civil war and famine were beginning to affect his closest collaborators, he never tired of pressing them to take a restful holiday, or consult a specialist, or take a cure, because the revolution needed strong and healthy men. Your health, he used to repeat, is public property which you are not allowed to squander. Gorky, whose attitude to Lenin after his death bordered somewhat on maudlin sentimentality, saw in this solicitude tenderness and love for a fellow human being; while Trotsky described it as a utilitarian concern with the great cause for which Lenin himself lived.

Lenin once remarked that there are musicians who have a sense of absolute pitch and there are others about whom one can say that they possess the sense of absolute 'revolutionary pitch': an example of such men was Marx, another was Chernyshevsky. One may add that such an absolute revolutionary pitch was innately Lenin's too, and Krupskaya may have had this in mind when she spoke about the 'something' that Lenin and Cherny-shevsky had in common.

Lenin first read the novel *What is to be Done?* when he was a boy of 14. It made no impression on him. But when he re-read it at the age of 18 he became, as he said, thoroughly transformed by it. He used an even more telling Russian idiom: he was completely 'ploughed over' by the book. The novel similarly affected most of his contemporaries. Who – asks Plekhanov – after having read this novel did not subject to the severest scrutiny his own life? 'To all of us the novel was a source of moral strength and of faith in a better future.' Plekhanov had no patience with the 'obscurantists' who discussed and criticised its construction or deplored its lack of artistic merit. 'But let them show us which one of the most outstanding, truly artistic works of Russian literature could be compared with *What is to be Done?* in its impact on the moral and intellectual development of [our] country?... Since the time when printing presses were established till this very day no published work achieved the success of Chernyshevsky's novel.'[8]

On the younger generation, the one following Lenin, the book did not exercise the same magic spell. Vera Zasulich tried in vain to convey to the 'young people of the 1900s', to whom Chernyshevsky's novel seemed 'dull and empty', the emotion with which she and her friends of the 1860s and 1870s had read it. To understand the wealth of ideas concealed behind the Aesopian language of the novel, a key was needed, a key which eluded the censorship but was the common property of the awakened intelligentsia.

Chernyshevsky wrote the novel in the most harrowing conditions. Thrown into the Peter and Paul fortress in July 1862, he immediately planned to produce 'something light, something popular, a kind of a novel, witty, descriptive ... so that even those to whom nothing else appeals but novels, should read it. ...' The most essential chapter (the thirty-third), devoted nearly entirely to Rakhmetov, was begun when Chernyshevsky was on hunger strike, the first hunger strike in the history of Russian political prisoners. This prisoner was indeed a giant of a man: iron chains on his feet, a dark and dank dungeon with its impenetrable walls did not prevent his mind from going out with 'something light' to those people who 'have just twaddle in their heads because they are poor, and pitiful, and bad and unhappy: it should be made clear to them where lies the truth and how they should think and live'.

That the novel, written in under four months, appeared in

print at all and so soon afterwards, was something of a miracle. The prison authorities, headed by Prince Galitzin, let the manuscript out of the fortress because, according to the letter of the law, there was nothing in it about the prisoner's conditions of life. The censor of the journal *Sovremennik*, which serialised the novel from February till May 1863, overawed by the signature of Prince Galitzin, let it pass without reading it. He lost his job subsequently and the book was banned; but by then nearly the whole of literate Russia was learning 'where lies the truth' and was drawing moral strength not only from the *dramatis personae* of the novel, but also from the tragic fate of its martyred author.

More than twenty years later young Vladimir Ulyanov during his enforced residence in the village of Kokushkino, read the yellowed pages of *Sovremennik*. By that time Chernyshevsky was a broken man – deranged and slowly dying in exile in Astrakhan. He never answered, perhaps never received, the admiring letter sent to him from Kokushkino. During his lifetime Lenin returned to the novel many times, remembering the slightest detail.[9]

It is now largely irrelevant whether *What is to be Done?* was a novel of a utopian socialist unusually distrustful of all liberal half-measures, or of a 'Marxist before Marx'. The fact is that he prepared – 'ploughed up' – the ground for the Marxism of the future which Lenin so fruitfully raised. The reason for the peculiar fascination which the novel had for Lenin should perhaps be sought as much in the affinity between the author and his devoted reader as in that between Rakhmetov – the hero and central idea of the story – and the personality of the young Ulyanov.

From the depths of the Peter and Paul fortress Chernyshevsky warned future fighters that they would need all their power of endurance in their struggle for freedom: Rakhmetov acquires Herculean strength, makes his body impervious to pain. (The picture of Chernyshevsky's hero sleeping on a bed of nails might have been greeted with derision by some 'obscurantist' literary critic but it was a grim warning to the revolutionaries of the 1860s and 1870s.) He is acquainted with all the fundamental works essential to his understanding of the coming revolution.

To the exclusion of all inessentials he devotes himself wholly to what is for him his life's purpose.

In Rakhmetov Chernyshevsky created the antithesis to Oblomov, the central figure of Goncharov's novel published in 1859. Oblomovism – indolence, lack of will and inertia – was the curse of Russian society and of those layers of the 'progressive' intelligentsia which, conscience-stricken and well-meaning, frittered away their indignation about the iniquities of the regime in long and futile palavers around steaming samovars. Against such a background Rakhmetov, with his concentration and discipline, stands out as a startling and unique figure. He was Russia's first professional revolutionary and his singleness of purpose must have quickened young Ulyanov's imagination and helped to mould his personality.

Lenin's taste in literature and the arts was extremely orthodox and, as if congealed in the nineteenth century (see pp. 123ff), 'Lenin had, throughout his life, very little time to devote to any systematic study of art, and always considered himself ignorant on these matters; and since he hated all dilettantism which was so alien to his nature, he disliked to express himself on the subject of the arts. Nonetheless, he had very definite tastes: he liked Russian classics, realism in literature and painting. . . .'[10]

He was steeped in the classics, both Russian and European, and in his speeches and writings made frequent references to Pushkin, Nekrasov, Lermontov, and Saltykov-Shchedryn. The works of Turgenev, all twelve volumes, were sent to him in exile in Shushenskoye; later on he asked for the same works of Turgenev in a German translation so that by comparing the two texts he could perfect his knowledge of German and learn the most subtle nuances of the language.* A volume of Nekrasov and Goethe's *Faust* were the two books which, apart from those dealing with economic problems, Lenin took with him on his first trip abroad. *Faust* he read and re-read in German in Siberia, and then, later on, in Russian in Paris.

* The load of books which Lenin accumulated in Shushenskoye and brought back from exile weighed nearly 5 cwt.

Naturally enough his taste in literature was determined and circumscribed by his intense interest in social questions and he was attracted by authors for whom these questions were equally relevant. His tastes were definite and he made no secret of them; yet in his private talks with friends and collaborators there was a slight note of embarrassment whenever questions of literature were discussed – they were touched upon rather than debated *au fond*. In public he was as reticent about his literary opinions as he was about his views on art, and he never assumed the role of a literary critic. When he wrote on Tolstoy, it was as a Marxist critic of Tolstoyanism, of a social and philosophical trend, which he tried to expose. He was fascinated by the contradictions in Tolstoy and he returned to them again and again.

To Lenin, Tolstoy was both a great revolutionary and a dangerous reactionary at the same time. This nobleman, with an extraordinarily sensitive conscience, was representing the wretched Russian peasantry in revolt against the double yoke of hypocritical Church and autocratic State. However, no matter how rebellious the peasantry might have been, it was unable by itself to carry the revolution to the end; it was amorphous, lacked class consciousness (or rather was permeated by false consciousness) and, sooner or later, was bound to slip back into obscurantism and religious prejudice. This ambivalence found its highest, its most concentrated and artistic expression in Tolstoy, who was himself shattering all the pillars of evil authority and yet kept preaching non-resistance to evil. Lenin had a boundless admiration for the breadth of Tolstoy's talent and sighed deeply over the poverty of his philosophy. He castigated those critics who saw Tolstoy as an aristocrat indulging in the luxury of 'doing good' and preaching Christian charity, as well as those who looked upon him as a new kind of Spartacus about to lead the slaves into battle against their masters.

Into this controversy between the critics Lenin stepped with a clear didactic purpose in mind: he was less concerned with the aesthetic or artistic analysis of Tolstoy's writings than with teaching his cadres to avoid facile and pseudo-Marxist schematisation and simplification, and to seek out the dialectical contradictions which do not detract from a writer's work, but so very often invigorate and refine his achievement.

Perhaps more than any other Bolshevik leader, Lenin was intensely conscious of the degree to which he himself, as a revolutionary internationalist, was rooted in Russia's traditions and was at the same time a product of Western culture. His distrust of modernistic trends in art and literature which exploded so colourfully and with such luxuriance on to the Russian scene right after 1917, was not only a matter of a different old-fashioned and conventional taste or lack of understanding, but also of a profound intellectual modesty. It is true, Lenin used to tell young audiences, that our achievement has been tremendous; it is true that the Bolshevik revolution will always remain one of the greatest landmarks in mankind's history. But we should not, as the young were inclined to do, claim all the merit for ourselves. The ground was prepared for us by generations of thinkers, ideologists, philosophers, writers, artists and martyrs; we stand on the shoulders of our fathers and forefathers and it would not do to kick them, claiming that because we are beginning to build quite a new proletarian order, all those who lived before us in the stuffy atmosphere of bourgeois society mean nothing to us. Has not Marxism developed as 'the direct and immediate continuation of the teachings of the greatest representatives of philosophy, political economy and socialism?' Isn't Marxism the legitimate successor to the best that man produced in the past? Culture cannot be contained or monopolised by one class or one nation at any one period of time. The awareness of the continuity of mankind's achievement is of paramount importance to all those who aspire to build a new social order.

To reject all that was old just because it was old and to welcome all that was new just because it was new, was a very dangerous principle, repeated Lenin. He warned the Young Communists, in his speech at the third Congress of their organisation, that no step forward could be made unless and until the present generation absorbed the world's cultural heritage.* It gives us a measure of the simplicity of his audience

* One may note, incidentally, how mistaken were those who sought in Leninism the legitimacy of the Chinese 'cultural revolution': Lenin would

that Lenin felt called upon to expound such obvious truths to it. And yet his words, bordering on clichés, were to many of his listeners a revelation which helped them to clear their confused minds. Alexander Zharov, the future poet, who as a 16-year-old member of the Comsomol was present at the Congress, described the excitement with which the delegates were gathering to hear Lenin. They expected a rousing call to action and were ready to march straight from the hall to join the ranks of the Red Army; they had a sense of anti-climax when they were told that the essential task of the young 'can be expressed in one word: to learn. . . . To learn ? ? ? And what about Wrangel who was still in the Crimea ?' They felt somewhat cheated of the glory of their dreams. 'We had been especially bewildered', says Zharov, 'by what attitude should we, the young, adopt towards "the old culture" which, we were told by some *litterateurs*, was nothing but "old rubbish", "old rags" worthy only of a scrapheap.'[11] And here he recalls a piece of poetry by V. Kirillov, apparently popular at the time:

We are rebelliously, passionately tipsy
Let them scream at us: 'Wreckers of beauty!'
In the name of our Tomorrow – we shall burn Raphael,
Destroy museums, and trample underfoot the arts.

No wonder that Lenin viewed with distrust the various attempts at creating a 'new culture' in a country where the 'old culture' has not as yet done its civilising work. It was arrogant, presumptuous, and futile, to try and build new artistic values – and this shaft was aimed at the Proletkult – rejecting the old ones with a contempt which testified only to a low level of education and lack of discrimination.

The Proletkult was formed in 1918 by a heterogeneous group of writers and artists of the 'new wave', some of whom accepted, and some of whom were soon to reject, the revolution. Among them were Acmeists, Futurists, Imagists, Formalists and a host of other more or less ephemeral schools, but they all pro-

have been horrified by the fierce offensive against all old ideas, culture, customs and habits proclaimed in Peking and Shanghai in the summer of 1966 and by the contemptuous denunciations of Balzac and Beethoven, Hugo and Shakespeare, and Pushkin and Chernyshevsky as the products of a rotting bourgeois culture.

claimed that a new epoch called for new forms in literature and art. To Lenin their style and experiments in artistic creation lacked appeal; moreover, he was shocked by their icono-clastic zeal and lack of intellectual discipline. It was Trotsky, the literary man, who, sharing Lenin's apprehension at the Proletkult's intolerance, was nevertheless prepared to defend their right to create new 'isms', and engaged in an exhaustive debate with the group. He pointed out that the aim of socialism was to create a classless society with unlimited scope for a universal culture in which by definition there would be no room for any 'class' culture. The intellectuals were no doubt stirred by the dynamic force of the revolution; they should not, however, mistake their rebellion against the dullness and stifling conformity of the pre-revolutionary atmosphere for an artistic counterpart of the great social upheaval. In this con-sisted their 'pseudo-Octobrism'.[12] They were justified, Trotsky maintained, when they strove to free themselves from the shackles of established and sanctified form and style, even if they indulged in experiments which at first produced obscure eccentricities. But when they addressed themselves to the working class with the cry 'Down with Tradition', they sadly misjudged reality: the working class possessed no literary or artistic tradition to shake off, and the call to 'burn Raphael' neither should, nor could, find an echo among the Russian proletariat, which knew nothing about Raphael or any other Italian master.

The literary trend which baffled Lenin more than any other was Futurism (see pp. 186ff). The Futurists were the most vociferous and aggressive, and also the most talented, of all the literary groups in the immediate post-revolutionary years. They called for a sharp break with all that was *passé*: not only with the paltry half-feudal, half-bourgeois culture of the old Russia, but with the 'ages of tradition' in every sphere of mankind's achievement. It was not an accident that in Italy they were attracted by the fascist movement which, though from a dia-metrically opposite end, expressed the same impatience with the political inertness of the bourgeoisie. They, the Futurists, were to be the torchbearers of the new age. Only futuristic art could represent the art of the proletariat with whom the future lay, their theorists insisted, quite oblivious of the plain fact that it was precisely their mode of expression which was utterly incomprehensible, even to the most advanced and educated Russian worker. In this they seemed to have been floating on Mayakovsky's 'cloud in trousers', very, very high above the ground. In their Manifestoes they insisted on some basic connection between art and technology. Their fondness for ultra-modern technical language reflected nothing else but Russia's backwardness and poverty: their dreams about skyscrapers and submarines, dirigibles and ferro-concrete seemed all the more poetic, because they were nearly as far from Russian reality as were the planets and the moon for romantic poets of the previous generation whose works they despised. When Mayakovsky enjoined his readers and listeners to 'toss the ferro-concrete into the sky', Lenin remarked quite unmoved: Why should we toss it into the sky if we so badly need it on our earth? (see p. 189). Trotsky, who was infinitely more responsive to the flights of pure fancy, appreciated Mayakovsky's *élan* and imagery, but was critical of his 'hyperbolic' style 'which out-thundered thunder'. Unlike Lenin, Trotsky held that the more Mayakovsky tried to be a good communist, the less good and artistic he was as a poet.

Lenin was all the more bewildered and irritated by the futuristic thunder and lightning, as in his own entourage the 'modernists' found a great deal of support and protection. Indeed, it needed 'courage' – as he told Klara Zetkin – to admit that he, Lenin, was a 'barbarian', because he neither understood nor enjoyed the works of Imagists, Cubists, Futurists or Formalists. In all humility he appealed to M. N. Pokrovsky, Lunacharsky's deputy in the Commissariat of Education, to help in the fight against Futurism. With Lunacharsky himself, who for a time patronised the Proletkult and other modern 'isms', it came to a clash over the printing of Mayakovsky's poem '150,000,000' in as many as five thousand copies (see p. 186). Lenin's rebuke to Lunacharsky was couched in the style in which he communicated with those that were closest to him: pithy, sharp, direct and undiplomatic. A few months later, on 10 November 1921, in language more formal but even more severe, Lenin reprimanded the State Publishing

House for having published his own essay on the 'Fourth Anniversary of the Revolution' in an extravagant edition of 50,000 and gave strict instructions to print no more than 5,000 copies of his new article 'On the Importance of Gold Now and After the Victory of Socialism'.[13]

Lenin's utilitarian-didactic attitude to art found its expression, sometimes slightly amusing, in his desire to 'embellish Moscow' and other cities and, by the same token, to stimulate revolutionary propaganda (see p. 200). He conceived a plan to replace street advertisements with large-scale revolutionary posters and also to erect, as soon as possible, huge 'monumental' statues and busts of precursors of socialism and freedom-fighters of previous centuries. The need for such 'embellishment' was to Lenin's mind so immediate, that the statues were to be made out of whatever material was available at the time, even plaster of Paris. He was 'utterly outraged' because his idea was apparently not taken up seriously or quickly enough. In the end, in spite of his impatient proddings, the 'monumental propaganda' proved to be a fiasco. The monuments were neither produced speedily enough nor when they were erected did they turn out to be anything more than transient. Having been cast not in bronze but in some flimsy clay which could not withstand the ravages of the weather, they soon crumbled, broke or just disappeared mysteriously.

Lunacharsky recalls the disarming bewilderment in the eyes of Lenin when, visiting with Kamenev an exhibition of models, he was asked to express his opinion on some modernistic sculpture: 'I do not understand anything here, ask Lunacharsky ...' was his answer. 'And I thought you might want to put up a futuristic monstrosity. . . .' He sighed with relief when he found that none of the exhibits were to Lunacharsky's liking either. 'Karl Marx Standing on Four Elephants' obviously baffled him beyond measure. But so little did he trust his own judgement that at the insistence of the sculptor (who was determined to get a prize), he used his influence to reconvene the jury. Luckily, 'Karl Marx Standing on Four Elephants' did not seem to have a chance. What Lenin was concerned with in sculpture or painting was in the first instance 'likeness' and realism: '. . . tell the artist that the head should be lifelike . . .'

This request must have been as embarrassing for Lunacharsky as it is for us today.[14]

The truth is that Lenin lacked visual imagination. While his taste in music and literature, classical and orthodox throughout his life, had been cultivated since early childhood in his parental home, visual arts seem not to have aroused any interest in the family circle. During his wanderings in exile he seems never to have gone to see any of the major art collections of Europe. There is no mention either of the Louvre or of the Tate Gallery in any of his letters home. He frankly admitted that he could not bear visiting museums and exhibitions, and to a young revolutionary who on arriving from Russia asked him what was worth seeing in Paris, he said: 'Go and look at the Wall of the Communards at Père Lachaise, at the Museum of the Revolution and at the Musée Gravin. From the artistic point of view people say it's not worth much. . . . Go to the Zoological Gardens – this would give you the feeling of having made a journey round the world. . . . As to museums, exhibitions and other things of this kind, ask Georges Plekhanov – he knows all of it through and through and will give you good advice.'[15]

A debate on commitment in literature, fashionable in the West in the 1950s and 1960s, would have seemed to Lenin completely incomprehensible. His whole personality was so geared towards one goal and so thoroughly absorbed by the movement towards that goal, that he would have been organically incapable of abstracting literature and art in any form from the 'commitment' which was for him supreme.* Moreover, any artistic expression devoid of social content seemed insignificant to him. This does not mean that he did not enjoy works of art seemingly *non-engagé* or beyond commitment – his emotions were profoundly stirred by Beethoven's sonatas – but there is no doubt that as time went on his 'tenseness towards the goal' increased, and all inessentials were jettisoned. A 'utilitarian' approach to art was also determined by a deep sense of social priorities, especially in the period of acute poverty: 'It is not

---

* Under 'literature' the Russians understand all forms of writing: political, economic, journalistic, etc., while *belles-lettres* is sometimes used to describe poetry, novels and fiction in particular.

right', maintained Lenin, 'to spend big money to support such an exquisite theatre [the Bolshoi], when we have not enough means for the upkeep of the most primitive village schools'.[16] At the same time when at a meeting a member of the government declared solemnly that 'at the present juncture the Workers' and Peasants' Republic has no need of the Bolshoi and Malyi Theatres because in their repertoire are such "bourgeois" works as *La Traviata, Carmen* and *Eugene Onegin*', Lenin remarked wryly: 'It seems to me . . . that [the speaker] has a somewhat naïve idea about the role and purpose of the theatre.'[17] To Lunacharsky, who pleaded for a subsidy for the Opera, Lenin answered 'winking slyly': 'Whatever you may say, opera and ballet are the leftovers of a purely landlordist culture!'[18]

It was not accidental that only in Russia ballet remained, after all, preserved intact in its classical form; it never was a subject of modernistic experiments and regained something of its 'tsarist' glory under Stalin. 'The exquisite' ballet and opera were not only luxuries which the new republic could ill-afford; to the whole progressive intelligentsia they were also symbols of the tsarist past, with its hateful, idle, and parasitic aristocracy speeding to the innumerable gala performances, where members of the audience eyed each other's uniforms, decorations, diamonds, and tiaras with the same, or even greater, interest with which they turned their attention to the stage. Opera and ballet – stage, wings and all – were something of a private domain of the tsars, reflecting the outward splendour of the court and being part of it. When in March the Bolsheviks seized the Kshesinskaya palace, public imagination was somewhat titillated by the event, incidental as it might have been.*

At the Opera the emperor and his court felt safe: on that glittering stage there was no room for subversive sentiments, while the theatre with its high drama or satire was always restive

---

* Kshesinskaya, the 'dynastic' court ballerina whose devotion to Terpsychore was as profitable as the devotion to male members of the Romanovs, had the palace built for her by Nicolas II when still heir to the throne. During the revolution, Bolshevik leaders harangued crowds day and night from its balcony now adorned by red banners.

and struggled to escape from autocracy's grip. The theatre was 'the great agitator' and the tsarist censorship was even more ruthless towards it than it was towards the printed word. The theatre enlightens; it has the power to impress an idea which conjures up a common bond between the members of the audience and creates a mood shared by all.* The theatre concentrates more oratorical power than the best speaker on the hustings can display, because it naturally uses artistic conventions which on the tribune would only evoke laughter or be treated as histrionics. From a stage on which lighting, costumes, make-up and music, all have a part to play, a good actor can carry the audience from trivialities to the limitless heights of dramatic experience; a gesture, or the lack of it, a word spoken or unspoken, can convey to the audience everything which the censor could hopefully have cut out of a play.

To Lenin the role and purpose of the theatre was precisely that of 'the great agitator, the collective tribune addressing a collective audience'. From the same standpoint he viewed the role of the cinema which had the added advantage of affecting a truly mass audience. 'For us', Lenin told Lunacharsky, 'the cinema is the most important of all art forms.' This brief remark, made in February 1922, has been quoted *ad nauseam*, especially during the Stalinist period when Soviet cinema reached its nadir. In 1922 it was technically so underdeveloped that its splendid, sudden, but short-lived blossoming could hardly have been foreseen. In 1921–2 the most talented director, Eisenstein, was still completely immersed in the Proletkult's Workers' Theatre, presenting in a highly eccentric manner highly eccentric plays by Proletkult writers. The cinema as art was nonexistent; and it is pathetic to read now all the trivial details of filming of educational and propaganda newsreel on peat production or electrification, which were referred to Lenin

---

* In our own, unrevolutionary times, a striking 'fraternisation' of the whole audience with the actors during Adriane Mouchkine's *1789* contributed greatly to the enthusiastic reception of the show.

Uninfluenced by Lenin's view on the Opera, the demonstrators who brought chaos to the Royal Danish Theatre on 14 October 1971, protested against the 'culture for rich minority as exemplified by the Opera'; they demanded that the State subsidised Royal Theatre be closed down (*The Times*, 16 October 1971).

in a correspondence dragging on for over a year-and-a-half. This long exchange of letters would seem grotesque, if it were not such a sad document testifying to Russia's backwardness and poverty.

Stalin, unlike Lenin, did not 'consider himself ignorant in matters of art and literature'. He never refrained from making public statements – which came down with the force of the tsarist *ukase* – on linguistics and biology, on the writing of history and economics; he intervened in the debate on biology; paintings he liked had to be admired by the whole nation; tunes he hummed were worked into orchestral compositions and symphonies and performed by the most gifted musicians in the country; easy rhymes pleased him, and he delighted in poems celebrating his own person. Certainly it could not have been said of him what Lunacharsky had said about Lenin: '. . . Vladimir Ilyich never made guiding principles out of his aesthetic likes and dislikes.'[19] This does not mean, however, that Lenin had no *political* 'guiding principles' on the attitude of party towards literature. The search for these 'guiding principles' led to his article, published on 13 November 1905, in the short-lived legal Bolshevik paper *Novaya Zhizn* of which fifteen issues out of twenty-seven were prohibited by the censor (see p. 158). The article has been quoted again and again in an effort to demonstrate how it led to transforming literature into nothing more than the handmaid of the ruling party. From their opposing point of view, both Stalinists and the adversaries of Bolshevism have used Lenin's text to prove 'how Leninism inevitably led to Stalinism'. Paradoxically, both sides to the controversy derived particular advantage from such a 'proof': the Stalinists representing themselves as the true heirs of Lenin; the anti-Bolsheviks demonstrating where the original sin of the oppression of literature lay. Both, in addition, managed to obscure matters by endowing Lenin's remarks, which should be analysed in their historical context, with universal validity for all times and circumstances.

Lenin returned from abroad on 8 November 1905. By that time the first revolutionary wave which had engulfed Russia at the beginning of the year was over. But the temper of the working masses was still hot. The clamour for better wages, shorter hours, for civil liberties and universal suffrage was shaking Russia. On 13 October the first elective body which represented the hitherto disenfranchised workers – the Soviet – had its first meeting and immediately gained an extraordinary authority. The general strike acquired an unprecedented vehemence. The tsar, fearing that the masses, having downed tools, might lift their hands to strangle the monarchy, hastily issued a Manifesto full of liberal promises. The promises proved hollow, yet the middle classes believed that they had got what they wanted: civil liberties and a Constitution. Knowing that they owed their 'victory' to the strike action of the proletariat, they in their turn took fright lest the workers press on with their demands, social and economic. Now they saw the tsar, divested of his absolutism, as their shield against the hot-tempered 'republican mob'. And they did put the brakes on. With repression from above, with the about-turn of the bourgeoisie, the spontaneous and unarmed revolution was finally stopped in its tracks.

Lenin missed the greatest part of the revolution which he later called the 'Dress Rehearsal'. He came to Petersburg when the Soviet – the first Soviet in history – was twenty-three days old and its whole life-span was to be no more than fifty days. He still felt the heat of the upheaval, although the flame was already out. Events moved fast.

Immediately after his return, Lenin still believed that the embattled proletariat had won 'half-freedom for Russia' and he was preparing himself and his party for a precarious yet legal existence within the framework of bourgeois society: 'We are now becoming a mass party all at once, changing abruptly to an open organisation', he wrote hopefully, too hopefully, between 8 November, the day he returned to Petersburg, and 13 November, when his words appeared in print.* Within this bourgeois society the feudal censorship which hitherto had stifled everything living in Russia would cease to operate. But

---

* These words confirm that during the 1905 revolution Lenin radically revised his conception of the party: no longer was it to remain a tightly knit small band of professional revolutionaries, but a mass party attracting and accepting 'some Christian elements . . . and even mystics'.

the party press would have to beware now of exchanging feudal captivity for the captivity of capital, careerism, and 'bourgeois-shopkeeper literary relations'. This is why party literature, says Lenin, has to be subjected to party control. 'Everyone is free to write and say whatever he likes, without any restrictions', but similar freedom must be granted to the party which is, after all, a voluntary association and must have the freedom to 'cleanse itself of people advocating anti-party views'. It is quite clear that Lenin was envisaging the activity of his party within a multi-party system. Faced with a possibility of finding in the new 'mass party' 'some Christian elements' and even 'some mystics', he was erecting barriers beyond which these 'inconsistent elements' should not be allowed to go. He was in fact saying: if you writers and journalists do not adhere to the programme of our party, leave it and join some other. As if forestalling future misunderstanding, Lenin also answered the prospective 'ardent champion of liberty' who was out to accuse him of wanting 'to impose collective control on such a delicate, individual matter as literary work', and stressed that it was *party*, that is *political* literature, that he had in mind.

Some fifteen years later, amid the cruelties of civil war and foreign intervention, Lenin's precept that 'everyone is free to write and say whatever he likes, without reservations' became quite untenable.*

It would be incongruous to compare the methods by which 'undesirable' writers were dealt with by Lenin and Stalin, because both the subjective and objective conditions of life and work of the two leaders differed as widely as did their general world outlook, their character and their personalities. Stalin proceeded ruthlessly against the slightest – real and imaginary – transgression of the orthodoxy he himself had imposed on the party and on the whole country; loss of freedom and loss of life were the punishment not only for advocating anti-party views,

---

* Nor could those who did not 'adhere to the programme of the [Bolshevik] party leave it and join some other': whether the Bolsheviks liked it or not, in the summer of 1918 the Soviet Union was well under way to a single party system and political censorship. Lenin, however, never went back on his principle of preserving freedom of speech *within* the party though once a firm decision had been taken, party discipline required absolute compliance with it.

but even for speaking up for the party in an idiom contrary to the prescribed one, different from that explicitly sanctified by him. Lenin had to defend his party and the young workers' state from hostile counter-revolutionary forces. He openly proclaimed that the party could not afford the luxury of freedom for its enemies either during the civil war with all its military terrors or during the New Economic Policy (N.E.P.), which was greeted by some as the thin wedge opening the door through which, they hoped, capitalism might return to Russia. Stalin made his bards sing the praises of joyful and free life precisely when he was depriving of freedom not just the enemies of the party but the party itself. In the late 1920s and in the 1930s recalcitrant and non-conformist writers were sent *en masse* to Siberia; after 1918 those who opposed the Soviet regime were asked, allowed or encouraged to leave the country, and many carried on their political activities in Western Europe or the United States, in an atmosphere so much more congenial to them.

The letter printed on page 182 throws an interesting light on the way in which Lenin proposed to treat 'the writers and professors who helped the counter-revolution'. Writing to Dzerzhinsky, who was then at the head of the G.P.U. (State security), Lenin tried to impress on him the need for 'a more thorough preparation' of the measures to be taken; he was anxious that no action against the counter-revolutionaries should be decided upon without the most detailed investigation based on the written opinion of Politbureau members and a number of communist intellectuals and experts; he remarked that at the G.P.U. the matter should be entrusted to 'an intelligent, educated and scrupulous man', that it should be 'judged more attentively', and he expressed doubts whether the Petersburg comrades were not too rash in suppressing the literary-scientific monthly *Novaya Rossiya*. Apparently Lenin's doubts were well founded: the decision of the Petrograd comrades was rescinded and the paper, after missing the July issue, reappeared in Moscow in August under the title *Rossiya*. For reasons which may be easily understood the letter to Dzerzhinsky remained unpublished for many, many years. It made its first appearance only in the fifth Russian edition of Lenin's writings published in 1965, and the English text was made public as late as 1970. The comparison

of the English text with its Russian original is in this instance
more than ever rewarding and illuminating: wherever Lenin
used the expression 'expulsion abroad' – and he used it three
times in a letter of some 350 words – it is rendered into English
as 'deportation', *tout court*. No matter how far technically or
legally 'deportation' is tantamount to 'expulsion abroad' the
word had certainly acquired a different connotation (and as if it
were a different emotional load) in an epoch so cruelly marked
by Stalinist wholesale deportations into the vastness of Russian
Siberia. The placing side by side of the two texts illustrates how
the change of method was reflected in style and idiom.

It was said at the beginning of this introduction that the most
striking characteristic of Lenin's personality was his singleness
of purpose and the relentless straining towards his goal to which
everything else was subordinated. There was no division
between his so-called private and public life, because in its
entirety his life was given over to his cause. In his voluminous
correspondence there are hardly any traces of what to our minds
would be a purely personal relationship, from which theoretical
or practical political questions would be completely excluded.*
In some respects his letters to Inessa Armand differ from all
other letters he wrote, not so much by their content or subject
matter, as by their tone and form.

She was, apart from the family, perhaps the only friend whom
Lenin addressed, for a period of time (up to September 1914),
in the second person singular which in Russian, even more than
in French, conveys a sense of intimacy and warmth of feeling.

Lenin met Inessa Armand in 1909 in Paris. She was much
involved with the work of the Russian revolutionary emigrés,
and became even more so after Lenin had left Paris and she
remained there as his confidante. Quite often, instructed by
him, she acted on his behalf. She also belonged to the team
lecturing at Lenin's Marxist school at Longjumeau.

Inessa Elizabeth Armand was born in 1875 in Paris of French
parents who were both stage artists. After the early death of her

* Apart perhaps from his *Letters to the Relatives* which are not included
here; they form a separate volume, No. 37, of the English edition of his
Collected Works.

father, she was taken to Russia by her aunt, a teacher of music and French. At the age of 18 she married a wealthy industrialist, also of French origin, but the marriage broke down ten years later and the couple separated by mutual agreement. Alexander Armand seemed to have been a man of unusual benevolence and generosity: for a considerable time he maintained the five children of the marriage as well as Inessa, and gave her a great deal of support when, drawn into the maelstrom of the 1905 revolution, she was arrested and deported to the Archangel province. At that time she was living with Alexander's younger brother, who died in 1909.

The photographs and the recollections of her contemporaries reveal her as a woman of captivating charm and beauty and of exceptional vitality. This daughter of a French opera singer and a French-Scottish theatre actress, was equally at home in French, Russian and English. Herself an accomplished musician, she seemed to have possessed some intensely theatrical qualities; and she must have brought into Lenin's life and into his staid household a sparkle of Latin temperament and of Parisian effervescence.

She was only five years younger than Lenin, yet in his letters to her there is that indulgent and forbearing tone in which a teacher or a much older brother would explain matters to a bright and promising girl-student. He was not only teaching her, but also boosting her self-confidence: 'I am sure that you [thou] belong to those people who develop, grow, get stronger and bolder when they occupy a post of responsibility . . .' he wrote to her just before an international conference in Brussels to which she went to deliver – 'in her excellent French' – his report on behalf of the Central Committee. He briefed her very thoroughly, warned her of all possible pitfalls, and, here and there, like a prompter, suggested a turn of phrase which might most effectively check any insolent debater (see p. 104).

The only problem on which there seemed to have been a disagreement between them was that of the 'defence of the fatherland', where, in September 1914, she tended for a time to adopt a somewhat pacifist position. For Lenin the question was of supreme importance: 'It would be most unpleasant for me if we differed on this.' He chided her for her 'formalistic' and 'non-historical' approach and patiently explained what was more than obvious to him and what he had already stated more than once in pamphlets and articles. Whether Inessa became genuinely convinced of the correctness of Lenin's attitude or not, she seemed to have adopted it as her own.

They conducted their exchange of letters in a mixture of Russian, French and English and this was not devoid of comic touches as when he ended a friendly note with the formal 'Yours truly' in English. There were accents of extreme tenderness and playfulness; and now and again there crept in a particularly soft and wistful note. In January 1917 he wrote to her nearly every day, or at least several times a week.

Any writer who would try to reconstruct on the basis of the existing material some sort of *un épisode romancé* in Lenin's life would be disappointed. The fourth Russian edition of Lenin's *Collected Works* contained barely a handful of letters to Inessa; at the beginning of the 1960s the editors overcame their reticence and included over seventy letters never published before. Reproduced in a short biography of Inessa is a concise, but revealing note Lenin jotted at the beginning of her fatal illness (see p. 120). It is an intensely moving document and shows Lenin exceptionally tender and gentle and also, to use the words of Mayakovsky, the poet he disliked so much, as the man 'most earthly of all who have lived on this earth of men'.

Inessa died in the Caucasus on 24 September 1920 during the cholera epidemic. She was only 45-years-old, but her resistance was weakened by recurrent tuberculosis which she had contracted previously in prison and exile. Her body was brought back to Moscow; last tributes were paid at the House of the Trade Unions. When the funeral *cortège* made its way in the grey light of a winter day, the 'shrunken' figure of the great leader followed the hearse to the Red Square where Inessa was laid to rest in the place of honour – by the Kremlin Wall.

It seems that Alexandra Kollontay, who spoke at the funeral, was somewhat carried away by her romantic imagination when she later maintained that Lenin could not survive long the shock of Inessa's death (see p. 122). Whatever his feelings, 'from the funeral he went straight back to his desk' and resumed work. In the evening he presided over the meeting of the Council of

People's Commissars: the same day or a day after he visited Klara Zetkin who had fallen ill; wrote the usual number of letters and read the usual number of State papers. He remained very active till the end of the year. At the beginning of 1921 he took a short holiday in Gorki. He returned to Moscow to his normal work and his days were, as always, crowded with meetings, speeches, conferences, talks with numerous delegations – foreign and Soviet – discussions and correspondence. In December 1921 he was prevailed upon to limit somewhat his activities and, for health reasons, to withdraw temporarily from the capital. His hitherto strong constitution was beginning to be affected by years of strenuous labour. In May 1922 he was struck with partial paralysis, and although in the summer his health improved for a time, it became obvious that soon, very soon, the reins of power would be slipping from his weakened hands. And so began the terrible months of his 'last struggle'.* They were filled with tremors and tensions incomparably more poignant and tragic than any personal loss could have been.

Engels once remarked that history is made in such a way that it becomes the result of conflicts of many individual wills, affected in their turn by a host of particular conditions of life. What finally emerges, therefore, is something that no one willed.[20] Between 1921 and 1923, after only a few years in power, Lenin seemed to have been struck with particular force by some of the frightening results – which 'no one willed' – of the historic action to which he devoted his whole life and his whole being. He became painfully aware of the deep gulf between the Marxist vision of revolutionary development and the sombre reality of the revolution in existence. For him, Marxism was a concept of an international socialist community; he had expected that the Russian October had opened a new era and was the first step to the attainment of such a community. A few years after October he stood at the head of a ravaged country, at last at peace, but still surrounded by hostile forces, with no hope of fraternal help from the international proletariat. Celebrating the third anniversary of the Russian uprising he stressed once again his international standpoint and considered

* See Moshe Lewin, *Lenin's Last Struggle* (London, 1968).

axiomatic that 'in one country it is impossible to accomplish such a thing as a socialist revolution.'* Not long after his death his successor elevated the slogan of 'socialism in a single country' to the dominant national theory and a mere doubt whether the building of socialism could be completed within the confines of a single state was treated as heresy to be hunted out with inquisitorial ferocity and punished by death.

Together with other Marxists, Lenin had firmly believed that socialism must be the task of the working class, or at least of its majority; he also assumed, as did all other Bolsheviks, that the majority of the working class having supported them in the revolution, would not withdraw their support in the task of post-revolutionary construction. He was to see the working class tired of the revolution, weary of the exertions of the civil war, apathetic, demoralised and dispersed. The gulf between the 'proletarian' party and what remained of the proletariat was growing; the communists were now 'but a drop in the ocean of the people' and the aspiration to build communism 'exclusively with communist hands' proved a childish dream. And there were not enough other hands eager and able to engage on the daunting task of socialist construction. In 1917 the Bolsheviks and their followers had risen to defeat the old order, the archaic social relations, the corruption, the inefficiency, and the wilfulness of the ruling class. Soon after their victory they saw the *mores* of the vanquished creeping back. *Les morts saisissaient les vifs*; the conquered were imposing their 'miserable culture' on the conquerors.

It seemed that Lenin became suddenly aware that the growing shadows of the past were acquiring substance and beginning to throttle new life. His own active life was nearing its end. In his country retreat, in Gorki, away from the daily pressures of office, he seems to have been brooding over his own past and over his country's future and he was seized by something akin to panic. Mingled with that panic was an acute sense of guilt. He used to be fond of repeating Engels's words that in the period of revolution just as many stupidities are committed as

* The quoted sentence appeared only in the first three Russian editions of Lenin's *Collected Works*; after 1935 it was omitted from the text. See *Sochinenitya*, Vol. 25 (Moscow, 1935), p. 474.

at any other time, and he was always ready openly to admit all the 'silly mistakes'. But this was the admission of human mistakes made by a self-confident and competent leader. The sense of guilt that got hold of Lenin as he lay on his death-bed in Gorki undermined his self-confidence and was more profound; it must have been all the more tormenting because of the awareness that now time was short. Could the mistakes be made good?

What have we achieved? What have we created? We have defeated the old order but the incubus is still there, with its accursed poverty of mind and body, its inefficiency and soulless bureaucratic routine, its chauvinism, its oppression and wilfulness. Where have we blundered? Have I done something I should not have done? What have I failed to do to prevent the terrible distortion of our 'workers' state'? Whither is our young republic going? And who is determining the direction in which it is going? Have I kept silent when I should have spoken? Such must have been the tumult of questions agitating Lenin's feverish mind and aggravating his sickness. Only a few weeks before his final paralysis he maintained that he was 'quite well'. His was a *'nervous illness,** of such a nature that sometimes he felt quite well, that is, his head quite clear, but sometimes felt worse'.[21]

In his statements, speeches and notes made in the last period of his activity expressions such as 'the fault is mine', 'I must correct another mistake of mine', 'I am to blame',[22] are repeated several times until they culminate in the solemn and profound statement of 30 December 1922: 'I am, it seems, strongly guilty before the workers of Russia . . .' (see p. 241). With this sense of guilt went an intense search for remedies for the way to drag Russia out of 'the swamp' into which she had descended barely five years after the revolution. How to combat the bureaucratic deformation? How to defeat the Great Russian chauvinism? How to educate the masses and how to educate the educators? A tremendous jump forward was made, but today our party is sick though it is not 'becoming senile yet'. 'When the objective state of affairs in Russia . . . called for a supremely bold, swift and determined onslaught on the enemy, we made

* Author's italics.

that onslaught. . . . By that we raised our revolution to a height hitherto unparalleled in the world. No power on earth . . . can annul the major gains of our revolution, for these are no longer our gains but historic gains', he said, trying to embolden his followers and lift their spirits after he had delivered a scathing attack on the 'huge bureaucratic machine, that gigantic heap'[23] which the communists, with their abysmally low culture, imagine they consciously direct somewhere, while in truth that machine, that heap, drags and controls them. Anyhow, the communists are only a drop carried and tossed by uncontrollable forces in the midst of the ocean of people: '. . . we must admit that at the present time the proletarian policy of the party is not determined by the character of its membership, but by the enormous undivided prestige enjoyed by the small group which might be called the Old Guard of the party.'[24] And here immediately a note of premonitory disquiet slipped in: 'A slight conflict within this group will be enough, if not to destroy this prestige, at all events to weaken the group to such a degree as to rob it of its power to determine policy' (see p. 235).

The fear of a split within the Old Guard had been growing in Lenin's mind and led him to dictate, at the end of December and on 4 January 1923, the notes which were in effect his last will and testament. He was offering the party guidance and suggested ways in which the responsibility for leadership should be spread wider among a greater number of men. One of the first measures to this effect should be an enlargement of the Central Committee of the party which should consist of as many as fifty or even a hundred members. This, he thought, was needed 'in order to raise the authority of the Central Committee, in order to insure serious work on the improvement of our apparatus, and also in order to avert the situations in which conflicts among small segments of the Central Committee might acquire a disproportionate importance in the fortunes of the party.'[25] Then he gave a brief characterisation of Stalin and Trotsky, 'the most eminent leaders of the present Central Committee', whom he clearly saw as the future antagonists in the conflict he so much feared. His advice to the party was given in a somewhat tentative tone, as if he were anxious to avoid any suspicion that he was dictating, from his exalted position, a definite course of action; the characterisation of Stalin and Trotsky was suggestive, but inconclusive and hesitant. Was Lenin doubting his own judgement? He had some reason to be uncertain: less than a few months before, on 28 March 1922, he had defended Stalin and praised him for the way he, Stalin, was dealing with the question of the various small nationalities of the Soviet Union: '. . . we need a man to whom the representatives of any of these nations [Turkestan, Caucasus, etc.] can go and discuss their difficulties in all detail. Where can we find such a man? I don't think Comrade Preobrazhensky could suggest any better candidate than Comrade Stalin?'[26]

In the meantime the dramatic and brutal clash between the Georgian Bolsheviks and the General Secretary came to light. Lenin realised that Stalin had been deceiving and cheating him, that the man to whom the representatives of the small national-ities were to come and talk was answering them in the 'language borrowed from tsardom'. Lenin seems to have been stunned by this discovery and, as if not quite prepared to acknowledge it yet, stated that Stalin, on becoming the General Secretary of the party, concentrated immeasurable power in his hands, and he, Lenin, was 'not sure that he will always know how to use that power with sufficient caution'. Ten days later the tentative 'I am not sure' hardened into certainty, and Lenin advised his followers to 'remove Stalin' from the post in which his rudeness was becoming unbearable.[27]

Lenin's message remained concealed from the Soviet people; they did not 'remove Stalin' who, till his death twenty-nine years later, was protected by that machine of power created to ensure the 'historic gains' of the revolution. The dreadful machine grew in his hands and vitiated the very aims it was to serve. Towards the end of Stalin's life the worst 'tsarist features' which Lenin so hated, reasserted themselves with a vengeance. Years and decades will have to pass before the 'major historic gains of the revolution' which 'no power on earth can annul' fully reassert themselves in the country which had hoped to open a new era of international socialist community.

To all for whom such a community is the supreme goal,

Lenin will remain one of the great leaders towering above all others. Although his name was 'hallowed', he himself canonised and invoked in empty liturgy, his revolutionary theory could not be 'robbed of its true *substance*' and deprived of 'its revolutionary soul'. Looked upon as a man, and not as a 'harmless icon', he acquires a new dimension, a new reality. He becomes more impressive and more inspiring in all his rich humanity, with his hesitations and doubts, his anxieties and warm emotions showing themselves clearly through the breaking crust of iconography in which Stalin tried in vain to smother him.

Tamara Deutscher

I WORK AND LEISURE

G. M. KZHIZHANOVSKY

THE SIBERIAN DEPORTEE I

His shortish figure in the humble peaked cap that was his usual
headgear could easily pass unnoticed in any factory district. A
pleasant, swarthy face, slightly oriental – this is about all that
one could have said about his outward appearance. In a peasant
coat Vladimir Ilyich would have merged as easily with any
peasant crowd in the Volga region. . . . However, the spiritual
essence of Vladimir Ilyich was revealed much more forcefully
in his contact with others than by his appearance. On many
occasions I went with him to meet people who could not have
known about him previously and each time I foresaw exactly
what would and did indeed happen. Invariably, wherever
Vladimir Ilyich went, and whatever the milieu, as long as his
visit was connected with a discussion of serious problems, you
could be sure that he would immediately become the centre of
general attention. He was never shrill or loud, but whatever he
said was so charged with meaning, so clearly expressed that the
exceptional gifts of a man who could speak in that manner
would become obvious to all. . . .

. . . There was his tremendous capacity for work, his exceptional
and varied talents (it was not surprising that he was the top
pupil at his school), and a great store of physical strength. It
may seem strange to read in various accounts so many references
to his powerful physique as these would not normally be in
keeping with a man of his size. Nevertheless the fact is that his
small, compact body throbbed not only with spiritual energy,
but also with the physical force of a sound, healthy, normal man.
I recollect that on one occasion, during the time of our exile in
Siberia, I told him the definition of a healthy human being
given by Albert Billroth, a famous surgeon of that time.
According to him the emotional reactions of a healthy person
were clear cut. Vladimir Ilyich liked this definition tremendously:

'This is it', he said, 'when a healthy man is hungry then he
is really hungry; when he is sleepy, then he will not start

worrying whether he has a soft bed to sleep on, and if he hates anyone, then it is real.'

I looked at the high colour of his cheeks and the brightness of his dark eyes and I thought: here indeed is the splendid image of a healthy human being. . . .

. . . One was struck by his incredible power of concentration and ability to work. . . . When in the corridors of the jail where we were both imprisoned [in 1896] . . . one would hear the wardens dragging heavy cases full of books, one knew that this load was meant for Lenin's cell. . . .

Whenever I watched Lenin poring over a book, I was always impressed by his ability to separate quickly chaff from grain. His process of reading, as well as of writing, was fast and testified to his habit of mental work, to his ability to concentrate. He seemed to be just scanning the book, and yet he immediately detected its strong and weak points. Reading a book which had passed previously through his hands, you willy-nilly adopted his point of view: the passages underlined by him, his exclamation marks, question marks, his expressive 'hm . . . hm . . .' were so suggestive that the trend of his thought became at once obvious to you. . . .

I think it was during the first year of exile that I managed, under some pretext, to spend a few weeks in Shushenskoye, and this period of close proximity to Vladimir Ilyich remained vivid in my memory. At that time he was still living alone. His day, thoughtfully planned to the last minute, consisted of long hours of solid work alternating with regular periods of much needed rest. It was in the mornings that he experienced quite an extraordinary abundance of vitality and energy and he was ready for a bout of wrestling or for a fight, and very often I would fall in with his mood and give him the full satisfaction by pitting my strength against his. Then after a brisk walk, we would begin our work. Special hours were set apart for writing, for the collection of statistical material from available sources, for reading philosophical and economic literature (Russian and foreign) and for relaxation – when we read novels.

We did receive newspapers but, of course, with a great delay, and in sizable batches. But Vladimir Ilyich very astutely devised a means of reading them in a systematic manner: he arranged them in such a way that he read one issue a day, taking into consideration the overall delay. This arrangement made him feel that he received the paper regularly, daily, though somewhat late. Whenever I tried to upset this order and maliciously picked out and read aloud news from subsequent issues, he blocked his ears and vehemently defended the advantages of his method.[1]

O. LEPESHINSKAYA

THE SIBERIAN DEPORTEE II

From Krasnoyarsk to Minusinsk we [the deportees] made our
way by boat.* In a large nine-berth cabin my cot was next to
Lenin's. I remember that one day we were both reading. I
could not help noticing the speed with which he turned the
pages of his book. I just managed to read five or six lines and
Ilyich was already turning a new page. I listened to the rustle of
pages being turned rhythmically. I looked up at the volume in
Lenin's hands. It was a book in a foreign language.

'Vladimir Ilyich,' I asked, 'what are you doing?'

'What do you mean? I am reading. . . .'

'Is that how you are reading?' I said. 'Are you really reading
or are you only scanning the book?'

'Of course, I am reading, and very attentively at that.'

'But can one read so quickly?' I asked in astonishment.

'Well, that's how it is. You are right. I do read very fast. But
I have to, I have trained myself in fast reading. I simply must
read a great deal and that is why I just cannot read slowly. . . .'

In conditions of exile Vladimir Ilyich preserved his usual *joie de
vivre*. . . . Able to work productively and with great energy,
Lenin knew also how to give his much preoccupied mind the
rest it needed and how to bring variety into the monotonous life
of the exile. For Ilyich rest consisted not just in doing nothing,
but in giving his muscles the necessary exercise, in loosening
every part of his vascular system, in making his heart beat
strongly and rhythmically, in forcing his lungs into a more
active condition, in a word, in stimulating his nerves and his
whole body into the physical state in which one enjoys the mere
fact of existence. At rest, Ilyich was as active and lively as he was
in the process of most strenuous work.

Sometimes I accompanied him in his favourite sport of
skating. Our group would scatter over the smooth icy surface
of the frozen river. Ilyich, vigorous and full of joy, was there

* March–April 1897.

first, calling aggressively: 'Hey, who is going for a race?' Our skates would cut into the ice. In front of everybody Ilyich, straining all his willpower and his muscles in order to win at any price, no matter how big the effort.[2(i)]

P. N. LEPESHINSKY

Lenin wrote just as he spoke. In speech as in writing his thought runs like a full lively stream, and the author does not stop even for a moment to consider the form in which his ideas pour out, never stops to admire the felicity of his own phrase, nor does he ever get embarrassed by some clumsiness of his expression.[2(ii)]

P. N. LEPESHINSKY

'*A KIND OF BARITONE*'

The few days granted to us, deportees, for our get-together to celebrate the New Year [1898] in Minusinsk passed with terrific speed. Chess, lively talk, discussions, walks, more chess games and – for a change – singing together in a choir. It should be stressed that singing was not the least part of our programme . . . Vladimir Ilyich brought into our vocal performances a quite particular passion and verve. When it came to our usual repertoire, he would get very angry and begin to order us about:

'Go to hell with your "Suuuch is her des – teee – nyy". . . . Let us do "With courage, comrades, we go on marching". . . .' And immediately, in order to avoid further parliamentary delays caused by debates about the choice of the song by which, to tell the truth, the rest of the company was already getting rather bored, Vladimir Ilyich would start singing in his somewhat hoarse and out-of-tune voice, in what can be described as a cross between baritone, bass and tenor:

> With courage, comrades, we go on marching
> Battle will temper our souls. . . .

And when it seemed to him that the others did not put sufficient emphasis on the most striking passages of the song, he would wave his fists energetically, tapping out the rhythm with his foot. Against all the rules of harmony and to Starkov's utter horror, he would strain his vocal cords to the utmost and render the parts he liked most by pitching the notes either too high or too low:

> And we shall raise over the earth
> The fraternal banner of toil. . . .

resounds his 'kind of baritone' drowning all the other voices. . . .

Lenin liked music very much. There was a time when nothing gave him greater pleasure and nothing was more conducive to a good rest from the work at the desk than listening to the singing of Comrade Gusev (Drabkin) or to P. A. Krasikov playing the violin to the piano accompaniment of Lidya Alexandrovna Fotieva. (My thoughts have turned now to the period of our emigré life of 1904–5.) Comrade Gusev . . . had quite a good, powerful and 'fruity' baritone; and to his beautiful recitative 'They-did-not-wed-us-in-a-church . . .' our entire Bolshevik family audience listened with bated breath, while Vladimir Ilyich, leaning back on the sofa, his arms around his lifted knees, seemed to be deeply buried in reflections and moods known only to himself. After Krasikov's violin had resounded with the clear and delightful tones of Tchaikovsky's *Barcarole*, Vladimir Ilyich was the first to applaud warmly and to demand with great insistence that Krasikov should play once more. . . .[3]

P. N. LEPESHINSKY

THE SPORTSMAN

Among all the outdoor sports, shooting was Lenin's favourite. The amount of game he used to bring back from his expeditions was usually minimal. The birds at which he aimed his deadly weapon nearly always had an opportunity to jeer at the art of this amateur marksman. But this in no way discouraged him. The instinct of a hunter was quite satisfied when he could steal cleverly towards his intended prey perched on a branch of a tree, when he could measure with his 'practised' eye the distance between the unfortunate woodcock and the muzzle of his gun, when he could savour with all his being the anticipation of his 'perfect' shot, without, however, worrying unduly when his feathery victim, after the 'deadly shot' was fired, would soar towards the blue sky and disappear into the brightness of the day instead of toppling head over heels to the ground.

Perhaps he did not find the main delight in the illusion of shooting exploits; the truth was that he liked nature. And one could clearly see with what enjoyment he marched over the thickets and marshes of Shushenskoye: here he was, hopping from mound to mound on his muscular legs, watching the frightened woodcock flying away right in front of the hunter's nose. . . .

More than on any other occasion, Lenin's 'sportsman's nature' showed itself in the playing of chess. . . .

The author of these lines is also one of the lovers of this game and recalls with the greatest pleasure the times when the monotony and dullness of exile in Kuragin were made bearable by the expectation of twice-weekly letters from Lenin with whom I played chess by correspondence. . . . When I first met Lenin in Minusinsk I was impatient to challenge him to a duel over the chessboard. . . . Soon the result was obvious: I plainly lost the first game. . . . The second and the third games ended just as badly for me. . . .

Damaging to my self-esteem as it was, there was no other way but to agree to play with a handicap: Ilyich would remove one of his pawns and in this way our chances would become a little more even. I remember among other games one which the three of us – I, Kzhizhanovsky and Starkov – played against Lenin.... [In the course of the game] Ilyich lost a piece and seemed in a tight spot. We were sure that victory was ours.... The *Entente* [that is the three of us] was already mocking the unlucky opponent and excitedly prattling about the great success of the clever move of White which proved so deadly for Black, without noticing that the opponent, allegedly defeated but not yet surrendering, was sitting over the chessboard immobile, like a stone statue with an expression of super-human concentration on his face. His enormous forehead with its characteristic 'Socratesian' bumps was covered with droplets of sweat; his head lowered over the chessboard, his eyes glued to the corner where the main battle was in progress.... Not a muscle stirred on that face as if carved in ivory, on those broad temples marked by tense bluish veins....

The legend has it that Archimedes, deeply absorbed in the solving of his geometrical problems, did not pay the slightest attention to a Roman soldier who was obviously on the point of attacking him. The scene reminded me of this. It was clear that if anyone would now raise a cry: 'Fire! Run, save yourself!', Lenin would not have batted an eyelid. At that particular moment his aim in life was not to surrender, but to hold his ground, not to admit defeat, not to capitulate but to emerge victorious from a very threatening situation.

The lightminded *Entente* noticed nothing. I was the first to raise the alarm.[4]

T. S. BOBROVSKAYA

IN GENEVA I

Downstairs was the kitchen and next to it a rather small room where Elizaveta Vasilyevna lived,* forever busy at her simple housekeeping. A wooden staircase led upstairs into two larger rooms. The furniture consisted of one large table in Lenin's room and a smaller one in Nadezhda Konstantinovna's room. In each room there was a plain iron bedstead covered with a rug, a few chairs and some roughly assembled bookshelves. Vladimir Ilyich's table was littered with newspaper cuttings, manuscripts, statistical records and tables.

Vladimir Ilyich wore a dark blue, loose Russian shirt which gave a peculiarly Russian look to his stocky figure. Altogether, the general character of the place did not accord well with the staid Swiss atmosphere. No wonder the sharp tongued 'Makar' had exclaimed on his first visit to the small house: 'There is a strong smell of Russia here! . . .'

I expected Vladimir Ilyich to tell me more than I had already heard from him at the Landolt Café, but as it turned out it was he who asked lots of questions, wanting to know even the minutest details of our party work in Russia; he was also very interested in the way we professional party workers managed to make use of our time in jail to get on with our reading, whenever books were available.

When I told him that while I was in the Kharkov prison in 1901 I managed to obtain *The Development of Capitalism in Russia*, which had been published legally under the name of Ilin, he was obviously very pleased but tried to hide his pleasure and began to tease me: 'Poor you, poor you, having to delve into my long boring tables in a prison cell. How I pity you.'

Vladimir Ilyich asked about every detail of the daily life of the Tver organisation. He was especially interested to hear that his pamphlet 'To the Village Poor' had proved extremely useful to us in consolidating our links with peasant circles, and this time he did not even try to conceal his pleasure.

* Krupskaya's mother.

One rather unimportant fact which I related to Vladimir Ilyich for the sake of interest prompted him to talk about the necessity of having a thorough knowledge of the milieu in which one was to operate. In the case of underground work this necessity was all the greater since party workers must take into account every detail, however insignificant, and be constantly on the alert.

The event which proved of such interest to Vladimir Ilyich had occurred shortly before my departure from Tver. We had sent an old experienced comrade to act as instructor to a village circle, but he was back the very next day with a sealed letter for the Tver Committee. In the letter the organiser of the circle asked the Committee in confidence not to send that propagandist to them again, for he was 'not one of us', he was 'a gentleman'. Proof of this was the fact that after spending the night in a peasant's hut, when he washed himself next morning, he produced from his pocket not only a piece of soap but also a toothbrush, with which he 'began to brush his teeth and this is how only gentlefolk wash, in the country we know nothing about such brushes'. Such was the cultural level of the village population in Tver province, which at that time was considered one of the 'advanced' provinces in tsarist Russia.[5]

IN GENEVA II

... When walking, Lenin never seemed to get tired. I remember exceptionally well one of our excursions. This was in the spring of 1904. I was already preparing to return to Russia, and as a farewell treat we decided that the three of us, Vladimir Ilyich, Nadezhda Konstantinovna and I, should go into the mountains. We took a steamer to Montreux. We visited the sombre Château of Chillon and Bonivard's cell, so beautifully described by Byron. . . . We saw the stone to which Bonivard was chained, and the inscription written in Byron's hand.

As we emerged from the dark vaults we were instantly dazzled by the bright sunshine and the wild, overpowering scenery. We felt we wanted some exercise and decided to climb to one of the snow-topped peaks. At first, the climb was easy and pleasant, but the higher we went the harder it became. It was decided that Nadezhda Konstantinovna should wait for us at the hotel.

To get to the top more quickly we left the path and climbed straight up the slope. With each step the climb became more difficult. Vladimir Ilyich strode briskly and confidently, chuckling at my efforts to keep up with him. After a while I was climbing on all fours, clutching at the snow which melted in my hands, but still managing to keep up with Vladimir Ilyich.

At last we reached the top. A limitless panorama stretched below, an indescribable display of colours. Before us, as on the palms of our hands, lay all the Earth's climatic belts, all types of vegetation; next to us the unbearable brightness of the snow; a little lower down the plants that grow in the North, further still the rich Alpine meadows and then the lush vegetation of the South. I felt in the mood for some high literature and was about to start reciting from Shakespeare or Byron when I looked at Vladimir Ilyich. He was sitting down, deep in thought. Suddenly he burst out: 'Hm, a fine mess the Mensheviks are making for us.'

When we started on our walk we agreed not to talk about the

Mensheviks, 'so as not to spoil the landscape'. And as long as Vladimir Ilyich was walking, he was full of fun and the joys of life, having obviously put out of his mind all thought of Mensheviks and Bundists. But he had only to sit down for a minute and his mind would revert to its usual train of thought.[6]

S. J. BAGOTSKY

IN CRACOW AND PORONIN

It was arranged that we should meet on the Planty, the wide boulevard encircling the centre of Cracow, opposite the main University entrance.

On the day of the Ulyanovs' arrival I came in good time and sat down facing the red brick building of the University.* It was a sunny summer day. Children were playing all around. Students, in small groups, were leaving the University. I intently observed the passers-by eagerly looking out for Lenin whom I had never seen before, but whom for some reason I imagined to be a tall broad-shouldered man with a black beard.

Half-an-hour had passed since the agreed time. The benches around me were filling up. On one nearby sat a middle-aged couple – the man in a bowler hat with a small beard and a modestly dressed woman. But I did not pay much attention to them. I became a little nervous and started walking up and down impatiently.

The woman got up and with some hesitancy asked:

'Excuse me, you are evidently waiting for somebody? Aren't you Bagotsky?'

'Then you are the Ulyanovs!' I exclaimed. 'We have been waiting quite a long time while we were sitting practically next to each other.'

We all laughed and shook hands.

Such was the beginning of my acquaintance with Vladimir Ilyich. He was quite unlike the image I had of him. Before me was a man of medium height, with slightly Mongolian features, and a small reddish beard. Lively, slightly blinking eyes, a cheerful smile and simplicity of behaviour immediately made me well disposed towards him.

The Ulyanovs had left their luggage at the station. We had to collect it and to think of a lodging for the first few days, until a suitable flat could be found. . . .

The Ulyanovs wanted to settle near the woods and the river,

* 23 or 24 June 1912.

but as simply and cheaply as possible. Such conditions could be obtained in Zvezhyniets, a working-class suburb of Cracow, not far from the Volski forest, by the Vistula. That was where we went. The flats there were rather primitive and the houses not a little dilapidated. In the end we found a flat of two rooms and a kitchen in a comparatively well-kept house, and the Ulyanovs decided to take it. Now it had to be furnished. Nadezhda Konstantinovna undertook to do this all by herself, hoping that her knowledge of Polish, which she had known as a child, would be adequate for this task.

Three days later I went to see them. The furniture was already there and everything stood in its place: two narrow iron bedsteads, two plain tables, a bookcase and some chairs; in the kitchen a small table and some stools. Books and newspapers were unpacked and spread on the tables and window sills. Vladimir Ilyich was busy writing and Nadezhda Konstantinovna invited me as the first visitor to tea in the new place.

Unwilling to disturb them in their work, I was reluctant to pay them another visit. But after a few days Vladimir Ilyich himself came on a bicycle and proposed that we should go to the Volski forest and have a bathe on the way as well.

The flat at the Zvezhyniets proved to be uncomfortable. It was too far from the railway station where Vladimir Ilyich had to go every day to send off his mail. At the Lubomirska Street, near the station, the Ulyanovs found another flat in a new house. The street was built up on one side only and their windows opened on a wide view of meadows stretching right up to the frontier. . . .

When the Ulyanovs moved to Lubomirska Street we became close neighbours and used to meet more often. This gave me a chance to observe Lenin's daily life. If before I knew him as a powerful theoretician, now I understood what a genius of an organiser he was. His exceptionally sensitive 'feel' of any political situation allowed him to gauge the political atmosphere and mood among the masses from factual details hardly noticed by others.

The Ulyanovs lived very modestly. Literary work was the main source of their income – a very irregular one. Tsarist censorship made the publishing of Lenin's writings in Russia difficult. He refused his mother's offers of financial help (she was receiving a widow's pension) and was even embarrassed by the small food parcels which his family was sending, assuring them that 'now there is no necessity. . . .' In extreme circumstances, and for a short time only, did he agree to receive fees from the party funds for his work. . . .

Vladimir Ilyich's working day was strictly arranged. He would get up at eight o'clock, and no matter what the weather was, would go for a short walk. . . .

About two o'clock there was a break for lunch. [At that time] Nadezhda Konstantinovna was doing the house-keeping. Her culinary talents did not produce outstanding results – she had other more important preoccupations. But Vladimir Ilyich was not difficult to please and used to remark jokingly that too often he had to eat 'burning-hot' meat, by which he meant stewed meat slightly burnt.

After lunch he went on with his work. About five o'clock there was a break for a walk or a bicycle ride out of town. In winter, instead of a walk there was skating. Who, seeing this cheerful, youthful and energetic skater, executing elaborate figures on the ice, would ever have thought that this was the great theoretician, the great leader of the revolutionary proletariat. . . .

In the evenings small groups of comrades sometimes gathered at the flat. . . .

Quite often Vladimir Ilyich proposed a game of chess. He used to play with great concentration and rarely left his opponent's mistakes unpunished. If his moves took a dangerous turn, he would become more serious, would stop joking, would think deeply and get out of the difficult situation. Those watching him could gather from his smile that he had already found a way of extricating himself. When he lost, he would jovially admit his defeat. He liked to explain where his particular fault lay and gave all due praise to the effective moves of his opponent. I was a much weaker player than V. I. and always derived great satisfaction if I managed to defeat him. Most of us had little idea of the theory of the game and this made our matches even more varied and original.

At the beginning of August I went to Makov, a little village about forty kilometres from Cracow, to spend the second part of my holiday. Before going away I explained to Vladimir Ilyich that Makov lies at the foot-hills of the Babya Mountain, from the top of which there was a wide view of the whole range of the Tatra peaks. Saying good-bye, Vladimir Ilyich added:

'I shall visit you and together we shall climb Babya Mountain.'

About two weeks later I saw Vladimir Ilyich coming up to my lodgings. He had come to Makov on his bicycle, tired and covered with dust, cursing the bad Galician roads.

One had to start on the expedition to the top of Babya Mountain in the early evening, so that half-way up one could spend the night in a tourist hut, locally know as *schronisko* – a shelter. We had tea and then stretched out on a hill near my home so that Vladimir Ilyich could have some rest after the journey. About six o'clock we had supper and cycled to the next village, Zavoya, right at the foot of the mountain. Having left the bicycles in a small restaurant, we set off along a sloping path. We soon reached the woods. It was getting darker. Unfortunately we had left our torches on the bicycles. The path zigzagged up. Wanting to shorten the way, Vladimir Ilyich suggested we should walk straight up. We were advancing fast, from time to time meeting the path, but then, suddenly, we noticed that it had disappeared. Having decided that it must be somewhere to our left, we turned left, but without success. We started looking for the path in all directions, but all in vain. There was nothing else to do but to keep on going up and up. It was dark, we moved slowly, stumbling against bushes and stumps. There was the danger that we might have to spend the night in the woods. Suddenly a light twinkled. We hurried up. Alas! this was the phosphorescent glow of a rotting tree. We went on. Again in the distance something shone. The light became clearer. Soon we could distinguish two windows. We found the door and entered a large room. On a large stove in the middle a big kettle was boiling, around it all sorts of tourists' crockery. At the table and on plank beds about ten people. On the floor open rucksacks. We were in the *schronisko* all right. After supper, we stretched out on the beds, and tired out went almost immediately to sleep, having managed to ask the watchman to wake us up at four o'clock in the morning.

In the morning, through my sleep, I heard Vladimir Ilyich's voice:

'It's already seven and we were not roused! We missed the sunrise!'

We called the watchman.

'But *panowie* [gentlemen – in Polish] look through the window,' he said smiling, 'such mist that nothing can be seen two steps from you. I thought you'd better have a sleep.'

And indeed, it was drizzling. Nothing could be seen except pale whirling mist. It made no sense to climb up. We kept on asking the watchman whether there was any hope of better weather. His answers were not encouraging: there would be no change before tomorrow.

And so our enterprise was doomed to failure. We could not wait till the next day because Vladimir Ilyich had to be in Cracow in the evening.

In the pouring rain we walked down, collected our bicycles in Zavoya, and, pedalling with difficulty along the waterlogged road, got to Makov. Our fiasco did not discourage Vladimir Ilyich.

'On my first free day I shall come again', he said on leaving.

And indeed, hardly two weeks passed and Vladimir Ilyich came to Makov (this time by train). We went on foot to Zavoya and from there reached the shelter without any mishap. We had our torches and this made the climb much easier.

The watchman greeted us as old friends and promised to wake us early, no matter what the weather was like. Four o'clock and again mist, but not as thick as it had been last time. According to the watchman, high on the top it might be quite clear.

We moved on, following red guide marks painted on rocks and stones. We reached the top but the mist was still persisting. We could see no more than a few yards ahead. We decided to wait and have breakfast in the meantime. After half-an-hour the mist began to lift, to thin out and in front of us a splendid view was unveiling. In the distance, lit up by the bright rays of the sun, a long range of the Tatra peaks as if suspended in the air; below everything wrapped in fog, like a blanket of thick foam.

Vladimir Ilyich was glowing:

'You see, our efforts were not in vain!'[7]

II LIKE ANY OTHER MAN?

M. N. POKROVSKY

LENIN AS A REVOLUTIONARY LEADER

I should like to concentrate on two questions which, it seems, have not been dealt with either in essays or in speeches – though to read all that has been written about Vladimir Ilyich in the recent period would be absolutely impossible. . . .

The first of the problems to which I would like to turn could be formulated thus: what actually made Lenin *The Leader*? We Marxists cannot view the individual as the maker of history. To us the individual is the instrument through which history acts. Perhaps in the future it might be possible to construct such 'instruments' scientifically, just as we now construct electric accumulators. But so far it is not. So far the instruments through which history is acting, the accumulators of social processes are brought into the world by nature. But what are the qualities which make a man fit to play the role of a leader? . . .

Now, when we are looking into the past, it seems to me that one of the basic characteristics of Lenin was his tremendous political courage. Political courage is not the same as bravery and defiance of danger. Among revolutionaries there has been no lack of brave people unafraid of the rope and the gallows or of Siberia. But these people were afraid of taking upon themselves the burden of great political decisions. It was always clear that Lenin never feared to take upon himself the responsibility for decisions, no matter how weighty. In this respect he would never shrink from any risk and took responsibility for moves which involved not only his person and the fate of his party, but also the fate of the whole country and, to a certain degree, the fate of world revolution. This was so peculiar a phenomenon that he always had to begin his action with a very small group of people, because only very few were bold enough and dared to follow him right from the start.

I should like to remind you of the story of the armed rising of 1904–5. The image of that past seems to us now, in retrospect, full of grandeur, but to some contemporaries it looked ridiculous:

a man, in a worn-out coat, sitting in Geneva, declared a life and death struggle – against whom? – against the Russian auto-cracy holding sway over a country of 120 million people, a country of hundreds of thousands of stool pigeons and millions of *knouts*. That man threw down his challenge. I remember the attitude of bourgeois professors who would not utter the word 'comrade' except with a smile of derision: 'What a fool! Any man following Lenin is one of those fools who think that in Russia one could organise an armed rising!' Lenin was not deterred by the sneers, nor was he overawed by the scale of the undertaking nor by the awareness that it might mean a call to spill blood and that bloodshed might indeed ensue. The first attempt was not successful, but Ilyich did not lose courage. There were many who, after December 1905, became hysterical and shouted that now nothing remained for Lenin to do but to shoot himself. But he did not shoot himself. True, the first attempt had failed – the second, the third might bring success. In February 1917 Lenin's tactic was vindicated – the tactic of a call to an armed rising.

This was one aspect of his political courage; there was also another.

The first revolution did not come off, and an ebb in revolu-tionary mood began. This provoked disagreements: are we facing a very short pause in revolutionary movement? Such was the feeling of the overwhelming majority of revolutionaries Or, are we facing a long interval demanding quite a different attitude?

Ilyich did not react at once. He pondered for about a year and then came to the conclusion that we had to reckon with a long interval.

... Well, here was the man who had called for an armed uprising and who now began to recommend that we should not do much more than read the journal *Rossiya* which carried the stenographic reports of the sessions of the State duma. What a shower of derision this brought upon his head! – and this time not from the bourgeoisie but from our own people! Who did not scoff at him, who did not sneer. 'He lost his magnetic powers – nothing, nothing of a revolutionary was left in him!' (so people said). ...

A similar situation repeated itself in connection with the Peace of Brest Litovsk. In the opinion of the Central Committee, Soviet Russia should have continued to wage a revolutionary war. That was the way we were conditioned to react. I had an extraordinary, a moving, even a tragic conversation at Brest with our soldiers kept in captivity by the Germans. They asked me how soon would they be able to return home.

'Comrades,' I said, 'arm yourselves with patience because this cannot happen for quite a time. The Germans propose to us conditions which are unacceptable. We just cannot go down on our knees before German imperialism. We shall fight on!' And imagine that these unhappy lads agreed to this. As I was leaving they were calling after me: 'Yes, yes, comrades, don't give in! We shall go on bearing our sufferings!'

We all knew that in such a revolutionary war most of us would perish. What we did not know was that Lenin, inside the Central Committee, was already protesting against the revolutionary phraseology; he was explaining that we had nothing to fight with and nothing to fight for, that the war would bring nothing except the defeat of Soviet Russia. The Central Committee's decision, taken at Lenin's initiative, to accept the German ultimatum, descended on us like a bolt from the blue. I remember I was so indignant that I just did not feel like approaching Lenin in the hall of the meeting and greeting him. It seemed to me that morally something terrible had happened. . . . And Lenin said: 'we shall not fight, we shall surrender.' For this, I repeat, tremendous political courage was needed, a tremendous conviction that there was no other way out.

In Petrograd there was a great deal of heroic animation among the workers who, *en masse*, registered as volunteers with the Red Army. Then I went to Moscow, took part in workers' meetings there. I quickly realised that the atmosphere was not even half as 'hot' as it was in Petrograd, that the Moscow proletariat was not ready for a revolutionary war. As to the peasants – it was not even worth considering them. It was clear that, whether Lenin's diplomatic line was correct or not – and the German revolution proved it to be correct – we had nothing to continue the war with. There was no possibility to continue the fight when the masses did not want to fight. Ilyich was profoundly right. And yet, in the higher echelons of the party the mood was such that a great deal of political courage was required to take upon oneself the responsibility for declaring, in the general atmosphere of a revolutionary war: No, comrades, we need peace at any price![1]

MEETING WITH KROPOTKIN

On 12 June 1917, that is after the February revolution, P. A. Kropotkin returned from England to Russia, to Petrograd, where he planned to settle down. Soon, however, he changed his mind and decided to live in Moscow.

One day – some time in 1918 – to my office at the Sovnarkom (Council of the People's Commissars) came a member of Kropotkin's family – I think it was his daughter – with her husband, and told me about all the trials and tribulations he was going through organising his life in Moscow. It was clear that somewhere there was some confusion; Peter Alexeevich, as a veteran of the revolution, had undoubtedly a full right, even in this chaotic revolutionary period, to be allotted permanent living quarters. In connection with these difficulties we renewed our old contacts.

I immediately informed Vladimir Ilyich about it all and he gave instructions that Kropotkin should be issued with a special document entitling him to take possession of a flat. I soon went to visit him to find out how he was faring. Our meeting was pleasant and cordial. Peter Alexeevich lived extremely modestly; his room was full of books, and the whole atmosphere spoke of his intense literary work.

At our first meeting he explained to me his attitude to the October revolution. When the revolution took place, he said, he had already reached his declining years and to his mind only people below the age of 40 should take an active part in revolutions. When I disagreed with him, remarking that our party members most experienced in the conspiratorial and revolutionary work were over 40, he answered: 'Well, for Russia that's how it is. Here even the 50-year-olds, or more, have remained excellent revolutionists. At my age it's different.'* However, he took very much to heart all the events of our complicated life and was sincerely distressed by the vicissitudes of the great proletarian movement and by the fact that Soviet Russia was

* Kropotkin was born in 1842.

surrounded by white-guardist and anti-Soviet enemies. He said: 'All contemporary political parties must remember that the October action of the proletariat, which led to the revolution, proved to everybody that a social revolution was possible. And this world conquest must be defended with all our strength. The Bolshevik party acted correctly in taking on the old and truly proletarian name of the Communist party. Even if the party does not achieve all its aims, it will still illumine the path, at least for a century, for all civilised countries. Its ideas will gradually be accepted, just as the world accepted the ideas of the French Revolution of the nineteenth century. And in this lies the great merit of October.' It should be recalled that in the summer of 1920 Kropotkin received a visit of a workers' delegation from England. He handed the delegates a long letter addressed to the 'workers of Western Europe', in which he wrote that 'the toilers of European countries and their friends of other social classes must persuade their governments first to abandon the idea of an armed intervention against Russia, in whatever form, whether open or masked, as armed help or as subsidies [to her enemies], and then to renew their relation with Russia.'

As a convinced anarchist, Kropotkin did not agree with the organisation of our Soviet State. He was in general an opponent of Party and State. But when one talked with him not about theory but about practice, he understood that without the authority of the State it was impossible to consolidate the achievements of the revolution. At our first meeting Peter Alexeevich questioned me: 'I was told that Vladimir Ilyich wrote an excellent book about the State which I have not yet read, in which he puts forward a prognosis that the State and its rule would in the end wither away. By this single shaft of light thrown boldly on the teaching of Marx, Vladimir Ilyich has earned the deepest respect, and the international proletariat will never forget this. I regard the October revolution as an attempt to lead to its logical conclusion what was begun in February; and as an endeavour to achieve the transition to communism and federalism.'

Life in Moscow of 1918 was hard. Peter Alexeevich accepted the proposal of his acquaintance Olsufer to move into his home in the village of Dmitrov. In the spring of 1918 he moved there with the Olsufer family into a four-room flat. From time to time he would come to Moscow and we used to meet on these occasions. Apart from this he used to write to Vladimir Ilyich and to me on many subjects. Although constantly ailing and feeling poorly, Peter Alexeevich still made an effort to take part in local social activity. He spoke at a teachers' meeting, took part in the congress of co-operative workers, and warmly supported the idea of setting up a regional museum.

I was trying to keep Vladimir Ilyich informed about Kropotkin's condition and about my talks with him. Vladimir Ilyich always looked upon Kropotkin with the greatest respect. He valued him especially highly as the author of the work on the French Revolution, spoke in great detail about the merits of this book, and stressed that Kropotkin when surveying the events of the French Revolution was the first to give proper attention to the activities of the masses and to underline the role and importance of craftsmen, workers and toilers in general. He considered Kropotkin's work a classic and insisted that it should be read and widely recommended. It was absolutely essential, he said, that it should be published in a large edition and distributed freely to all libraries in Soviet Russia.

During one of our conversations Vladimir Ilyich expressed the wish to meet Peter Alexeevich. At the end of April 1919 I wrote to Kropotkin saying *inter alia*: '. . . Vl. Il., who sends you his greetings, told me that he would be glad to see you. If you plan to come to Moscow, notify us of the time of your arrival – I should also like to see you. . . .' Soon I visited him in Moscow . . . and he said that, naturally, he would also very much like to see Lenin. 'I have many things to talk over with him', he added.

We agreed that I would let him know over the phone about the day and time of the meeting, which I proposed to arrange in my flat in the Kremlin. All this happened at the beginning of May 1919 and I am almost sure that the meeting took place between 8 and 10 May. Vladimir Ilyich was to arrive about 5 p.m., that is after Sovnarkom office hours. I phoned Peter Alexeevich and sent a car to fetch him. Vladimir Ilyich was the first to arrive. We talked about the activities of revolutionaries of the preceding epochs. He said something to the effect that undoubtedly the time would come when we would publish the writings of Russian revolutionaries now living abroad. Vladimir Ilyich took from my shelves first one then another of Kropotkin's or Bakunin's books, and looked through them quickly page after page. At that moment Kropotkin arrived and I went out to meet him. He was slowly climbing up our winding staircase. Vladimir Ilyich strode along the corridor and with a happy smile warmly greeted Peter Alexeevich, took him under his arm, gently led him into the room and seated him in an armchair. He himself sat at the opposite side of the table.

Peter Alexeevich's face lit up: 'How glad I am to see you, Vladimir Ilyich. We differ in our points of view, we have differences about a whole series of questions on methods of action and organisation, but our aims are the same and what you and your comrades do in the name of communism is very close to my aging heart and brings me joy. And yet I am for co-operatives and you block them!'

'But we are for them!' exclaimed Vladimir Ilyich. 'What we are against are those co-operatives that conceal kulaks, land-owners, traders and, in general, private capital. We only want to unmask the pseudo-co-operatives and give the broad masses an opportunity to join genuine co-operatives.'

'With this I shall not quarrel', answered Kropotkin. 'Against such cases one should fight with all one's strength, just as one should fight against any lie and mystification. We need no camouflage and we should expose every lie; and yet in Dmitrov I quite often see a co-operative harassed, though it has nothing in common with things you mentioned before, but only because the local authorities, perhaps even people who yester-day were revolutionaries, changed as all authorities do, into bureaucrats, into officials, who want to twist their subor-dinates and who think that the whole population is subordin-ated to them.'

'We are against officialdom always and everywhere', said Vladimir Ilyich. 'We are against bureaucrats and bureau-cratisation, and we must pull up bureacracy by its roots if it still nestles in our new system. But you know perfectly well that it is extremely difficult to remake people and that, as Marx used to say, the most inaccessible fortress is the human skull.

We take all possible measures to achieve success in this struggle – life itself is the teacher to many. Of course, the country bears the heavy stamp of the lack of culture, of illiteracy, of backwardness, but nobody can blame us as a party, as a government, for what is badly done by the apparatus, especially in the depths of the country, far from the centre.'

'All this does not make life easier for those who are dependent on this unenlightened authority', exclaimed Kropotkin. 'Authority poisons everybody who takes authority on himself.'

'This you cannot help', added Vladimir Ilyich. 'You cannot make a revolution in white gloves. We know perfectly well that we have made, and are still making, many mistakes; we correct all that can be corrected; we admit our mistakes – which sometimes result from plain stupidity. In spite of all the mistakes, we shall lead our revolution to a victorious conclusion. And you, you should help us, let us know when you see that something is wrong; you can be assured that we shall welcome your remarks with the greatest attention.'

'Neither I nor anybody else would refuse to help you and your comrades in whatever we can. . . . We shall inform you of any irregularities which occur and under which people groan in many places. . . .'

'What you hear is not groaning, but rather the hue and cry of counter-revolutionary resistance to which we shall give no quarter. . . .'

'Well, and you say that one cannot do without authority', Kropotkin started theorising again, 'and I say that one can. . . . Just look how the beginnings of "no-authority" are gaining ground. For example, in England – I was just informed – in one of the English ports the dockers organised a wonderful, completely free co-operative, to which flock more and more workers from various other industries. The co-operative movement is enormous and extremely significant. . . .'

I looked at Vladimir Ilyich – there was a slightly mocking twinkle in his eyes. He listened carefully to what Kropotkin was saying and somehow could not understand how, after such a revolutionary flare-up as our October revolution, one could go on and on about co-operatives. And Peter Alexeevich continued telling us that somewhere else in England co-operatives were set up; and in a third place, in Spain, people organised a small (co-operative) federation, and how the syndicalist movement develops in France. . . . 'This is all wrong', Vladimir Ilyich could not hold back any longer, 'this disregard for the political side of life; all this only beguiles the working masses and diverts them from direct struggle. . . .'

'But the professional movement embraces millions and is in itself a tremendous factor', said Kropotkin becoming agitated, 'and together with the co-operative movement it marks an enormous step forward.'

'All this is excellent', interrupted Vladimir Ilyich. 'Of course the co-operative movement is important, only as syndicalism is it harmful. What is its main point? Can it lead anywhere? To anything new? Do you really believe that the capitalist world will give way when confronted with the co-operative movement? Oh no, it will try by every possible means to take it into its own hands. The same bunch of English workers who have joined the co-operative of "no-authority" will be crushed and made into the servants of capital, will become dependent on it and caught in a cobweb, in which capital, by a thousand threads, will tie up all that is new and so attractive to you in the co-operative movement. Excuse me, but this is just empty verbiage, trifles; what is needed is the direct action of the masses, and as long as there is no such action one cannot even talk about federalism or communism, or about social revolution. This is all childish prattle, empty talk, without any basis in reality, without power, without means, hardly moving us any nearer to our socialist goals.'

Vladimir Ilyich was standing up and speaking clearly, distinctly and with fervour. Peter Alexeevich was leaning back in his chair; he listened carefully to Lenin's fiery words, and then ceased talking about co-operatives.

'Yes, you are right', he said. 'In no country will it go without a struggle, without a most desperate struggle. . . .'

'A mass struggle', added Vladimir Ilyich. 'We do not need individual terroristic attempts and this the anarchists should have understood long ago. Only with the masses, through the masses and with the masses. . . . All other methods, including those of the anarchists, have been relegated to the limbo of history – nobody needs them, they are no good, and they do not attract anybody – they may only demoralise people who in one way or another have been drawn on to that old worn-out path. . . .'

Vladimir Ilyich stopped suddenly, smiled kindly and said:

'Forgive me, I must have tired you out. I have let myself be carried away. But we, Bolsheviks, we are all alike: this is our problem, our hobby-horse, so close to us – about these things we just cannot talk calmly.'

'No, no', protested Kropotkin. 'If you and your comrades think that way, and if they do not get drunk with power and feel there is no danger that they might become enslaved by the State, then they will achieve a great deal. Then revolution is really secure in their hands.'

'We shall try', answered Lenin jovially.

'We need enlightened masses,' said Vladimir Ilyich, 'and it would be good if, for example, your book on the Great French Revolution were published in a very large edition. This book is so useful to all.'

'But who would publish it? I cannot let the State Publishing House do it. . . .'

'No, no', Lenin interrupted, smiling slyly. 'Why of course not the State Publishing House, but a co-operative publisher. . . .'

Peter Alexeevich approvingly nodded his head.

'Oh, well,' he said, obviously delighted with the praise and the proposal, 'if you find the book interesting and valuable, I agree to have it published in a cheap edition. Perhaps one could find such a co-operative enterprise. . . .'

'One can find it, one certainly can,' nodded Lenin, 'I am sure of this. . . .'

On this the conversation seemed to peter out. Vladimir Ilyich looked at his watch and said he had to get ready for a conference at the Sovnarkom. He said good-bye to Peter Alexeevich very warmly and assured him that he would always be pleased to receive his letters.[2]

V. D. BONCH-BRUEVICH

KROPOTKIN'S DEATH

In the morning of 19 January 1921 I learnt that Kropotkin had fallen very ill – he had had two very severe heart attacks. I immediately passed this sad news to Lenin, who asked me to give the sick man all possible assistance; he himself ordered that two extra trains for Dmitrovo should be put at our disposal. I got in touch with the Health Commissar N. A. Semashko; a list of specialists for a consultation was drawn up. . . .

Together with Semashko and the specialists we went in two cars to the station where the railway authorities had prepared for us a train consisting of two carriages. We started immediately and soon arrived at Dmitrovo where we were met by representatives of the local party. When they learnt that we had all come to visit P. A. Kropotkin, and, moreover, that we came at the explicit request of the Chairman of the People's Commissars, V. I. Lenin, their astonishment was immense.

It turned out that the local officials were intensely prejudiced against Kropotkin. As an old revolutionary he was completely unknown to them; nor were they aware of his merits as a great writer, as a scientist-geographer, or theoretician of anarchism. The fact that in Dmitrovo there lived, in the house of an old nobleman, a former prince who for some reason was greatly helped, only irritated local officialdom. And as Peter Alexeevich used to be quite outspoken in his criticism of many things that went on in this backwater during these stormy years, it was understandable that the relations between the authorities and Kropotkin were strained, and sometimes even quite hostile. And so I had to enter into a detailed explanation of Kropotkin's role and activities, to make them see why Lenin was lavishing so much care and attention on the old man. . . .

The Moscow consultants diagnosed severe pneumonia. Peter Alexeevich seemed lively, his eyes were clear and thoughtful, and his speech unimpaired, but because of his age – he was 78 – there was danger and anxiety. His heart was not bad just then, and his pulse regular, but what next? He was assured of all that good nursing and medical care could provide. . . .

We returned to Moscow late at night. Next morning I sent a letter to Vladimir Ilyich describing all I had seen in Kropotkin's home. Here is what I wrote:

'Dear Vladimir Ilyich,

I went yesterday together with Semashko and other consultants to Kropotkin. The old man was very moved by our solicitude. The state of his health is grave and he is suffering. *Angina pectoris* of which an attack may last four to six hours, makes him choke terribly and gives him a pain in the heart and in the left arm. This is aggravated by quite severe, though so far localised, pneumonia. His temperature is 38·9. His pulse is normal without extrasystolics. The doctors warned that in view of his advanced age one can expect anything. However, we have immediately to provide Kropotkin with proper nourishment. He must not eat black bread and there was no white flour in the house at all. He needs semolina and potato flour for making *kissiel*, and so on. I am enclosing a list of what is needed. They have no kerosene and consequently no light. (Yesterday they got just a little with difficulty.) He must have milk; they do have a cow, but there is nothing to feed it with and the animal is half dead. Fodder must be provided. All this can be arranged, because the quantities are ridiculously small. We should also take over the cost of wood and the cost of delivery – they just had to pay 67,000 roubles for bringing in wood; this is quite beyond their means, and they were obliged to sell their last treasures. . . .'

On the following day all the provisions on the list, personally approved and signed by Lenin, were sent by a fast train to Dmitrov. A special Kremlin messenger was assigned to ensure a safe delivery of all the goods to the Kropotkins. . . .

During the night of 7–8 February at 3.40 a.m. we received the following cable from Dmitrov: 'P. A. Kropotkin died peace-

fully at 3.10 a.m. The cause of death: drastic weakening of
heart activity. . . .'

Kropotkin's remains were placed in the large Hall of Columns
of the House of Trade Unions where the public was given the
opportunity to pay him their last respects.[3]

30 September 1913

Dear A.M.,

... What you write about your illness worries me terribly. Are you doing the right thing living without treatment on Capri? The Germans have excellent sanatoria (for example, at St Blasien, near Switzerland) where they treat and *completely* cure lung diseases, achieve *complete* healing, feed you, then systematically accustom you to cold, harden you against catching cold, and turn out fit people, able to work.

While you, after Capri, and in winter, want to go to Russia? I am terribly afraid that this will injure your health and undermine your working capacity. Are there *first-class* doctors in that Italy of yours?

Really, go and visit some first-class doctor in Switzerland (I can find names and addresses) or Germany, and set about a couple of months of *serious* treatment in a *good* sanatorium. Because to squander official property, i.e. to go on being ill and undermining your working capacity, is something quite intolerable in every respect. ...

Yours,

Lenin[4]

V. D. BONCH-BRUEVICH

'*NO RHETORIC, PLEASE* . . .'*

Vladimir Ilyich, tired and obviously very moved by the whole reception which he did not expect . . . was trying to snatch a little rest; he kept asking about the latest events, about work and the organisation. Big crowds outside demanded speeches. Some comrades were addressing them from the balcony. Vladimir Ilyich moved towards the balcony, wanting no doubt to hear what our agitators were telling the people. He listened very attentively, sometimes approvingly, sometimes with a smile, murmuring his favourite: 'Hm hm!' which meant that something was not in order, rather doubtful, not quite right. . . . When at some point a very nervous, nearly hysterical comrade started, in a broken voice, to call on the crowd to get ready for an immediate rising, and to rattle off unending anarchistic phrases amounting to nothing, Vladimir Ilyich asked:

'Who is it speaking?'

When he was told the speaker's name, he remarked with a grin:

'Is he also a Bolshevik?'

Just then the man tried especially hard to gain glory, waving his arms with great force. Wriggling and twisting his whole body, he bellowed in a voice strained to the utmost, kept piling one resounding appeal upon another, battering, devastating, calling, cajoling. . . .

'No, that's impossible', said Vladimir Ilyich. 'He should be stopped immediately. . . . This is some sort of leftish twaddle', he concluded unexpectedly.

At last the orator was stopped and, in a state of collapse from fatigue, entered the room obviously waiting full of hope for Vladimir Ilyich's approval.

* On 3 April 1917 Lenin returned in the famous 'sealed train' from Switzerland to Russia. Unexpectedly for him he was greeted at the Finland Station in Petersburg not only by crowds of workers, sailors and soldiers, but by a ceremonial welcoming committee and a military guard complete with a band paying him full military honours.

Vladimir Ilyich said nothing and there was an embarrassing silence in the room.

The orator could not stand this; he wiped the sweat which was flowing abundantly from his face and head, turned towards Vladimir Ilyich and gushed with a terrific speed:

'An enormous amount of work. . . . One has to harangue the crowd like this perhaps twenty times a day. . . .'

'Twenty times! . . . Hm . . .', said Vladimir Ilyich slowly with a smile. 'No comrade, you should not torture yourself like this. . . . You should not. You'll make yourself quite ill. . . . You should take care of yourself. . . . All this is not necessary . . . rhetoric . . . shouting. . . .'

'Excuse me', the orator excitedly went over to the attack, 'but this is the most genuine Bolshevism, and here, they . . .' pointing at the comrades present in the room, 'they do not agree with me, they even swear at me. . . .'

Vladimir Ilyich leaned back against his chair and laughed infectiously.

'They swear at you, you say. . . . Well, one should not swear. What for ? . . . They do not agree, you say. . . . Well, very well. . . . Comrades,' he said suddenly in a business-like manner turning to the members of the [Bolshevik] Committee, 'it's no good scolding him. You must give him a period of rest and then assign him to some other work – yes, transfer him' – this last word was stressed – 'transfer him to a job that requires much less speech-making', Vladimir Ilyich added, moving to another room.[5]

V. D. BONCH-BRUEVICH

CULT OF PERSONALITY*

... About ten o'clock Lenin came to his room and immediately started looking through the newspapers. Less than half an hour later I heard his bell being rung anxiously several times. Fearing that something might have happened, I jumped up and ran into his office. On entering I saw Vladimir Ilyich: he went very pale, was obviously very agitated, and turned to me reproachfully.

'What is this? How could you have allowed this? See what they write in the newspapers . . . ? It's shameful. They write about me, that I am like this and like that and so on, exaggerating everything, calling me a genius, a kind of extraordinary man – there is an element of mysticism in all this. . . . Collectively *they* wish, *they* demand, *they* request that I should regain my health. . . . In this way they will end up by offering prayers for my return to health. . . . But this is terrible. . . . Where does it come from? All our lives we fought against exalting the individual, against the elevation of the single person, and long ago we were over and done with the business of an [individual] hero, and here it comes up again: the glorification of one personality. This is not good at all. I am just like everybody else. . . . I am treated by the best doctors. Well, what's more . . . the mass of our population does not have the benefit of so much attention, such good medical care and treatment, because we have not yet been able to secure all this. And here they single me out in such a way . . . this is terrible.'

I could not say a thing while Lenin was speaking with such vehemence, fearing that so much excitement might greatly harm him. When he finished talking, I said quietly that people really loved him devotedly . . . that our office, and I personally, received an unending flood of inquiries, letters, telephone calls, telegrams, a great number of delegations from factories, plants, unions; everybody wanted to know about the state of his health;

---

* On 30 August 1918 Lenin was shot and wounded by F. Kaplan, a social revolutionary terrorist. His convalescence lasted over two weeks. In the middle of September he resumed work in his office.

this widespread desire of workers, peasants, soldiers and sailors who decided to send a detachment of armed guards from the military fleet for his personal protection – all this finds its reflection in newspapers, in journalistic articles, in reports, letters and resolutions of workers' collectives.

'All this is extremely moving. . . . I did not know that I gave rise to so much apprehension and anxiety everywhere. . . . But now one should put a halt to this without offending anybody. This is superfluous and harmful, and goes against our conviction and our view on the role of personality. . . . You know what – get in touch with Olminsky and Lepeshinsky. . . . I would ask the three of you to make a tour of editorial offices, of large and small newspapers and journals, and pass on the following message from me: would they, please, in a tactful manner stop all this and fill the pages of their publications with stuff that is more needed and more interesting ? Be so good as to do this for me as soon as possible.'

And Vladimir Ilyich returned to his writing.[6]

LENIN ROBBED

All this happened on 19 January 1919. Winter was severe that year and there were snow-storms over Moscow. The streets were full of pot-holes and mounds of snow were piled up on the sides. On that memorable Sunday we were going to Sokolniki to visit N. K. Krupskaya, who was on a holiday in one of the schools in the forest. They were waiting impatiently for Vladimir Ilyich as the children there were having a party that evening. We did not drive through the Red Gate but by the Orlikov road. A few yards from Kalanchev Square we suddenly heard an ominous shout:

'Halt!'

It was a man in a soldier's greatcoat. I pressed the accelerator and followed the bending road at speed. Vladimir Ilyich asked:

'What was that?'

I answered that someone, probably a drunk, was trying to stop us. We passed safely by the railway station, and when we were approaching the Kalinkins plant several men, revolvers in their hands, jumped into the middle of the road.

'Halt! Stop the car!'

Seeing that they did not wear the uniforms of the patrol detachments, I went straight at them. Another shout:

'Stop or we fire!'

I meant to drive on, but Vladimir Ilyich, thinking they were militiamen, told me to stop.

Coming to the bridge I put the brakes on. The car stopped. Pointing their revolvers excitedly they surrounded us and ordered:

'Get out! Quick!'

Vladimir Ilyich opened the door:

'What's the matter?', he asked.

One of the attackers bellowed:

'Get out! Shut up!'

He grabbed Vladimir Ilyich by his sleeve and pulled him out. Completely baffled, Ilyich repeated:

'What's the matter, comrades? Who are you?', and he reached to get out his pass.

Maria Ilyichna (Lenin's sister) and Com. Chebanov also got out of the car, without understanding what was going on. Two robbers stood on either side of Vladimir Ilyich pointing their revolvers at his forehead.

'Don't move!'

Another man, facing Vladimir Ilyich, grabbed the lapels of his coat drawing them aside with a swift professional gesture, pulled out of the pocket of his jacket a wallet with documents and a small Browning.

I remained all the time behind the steering wheel with my pistol cocked. I had to restrain myself not to shoot. My shot might have hit one or two robbers, but inevitably it would have ended by them firing at us. I could not risk this.

Maria Ilyichna, still not realising that these were real bandits, turned towards them angrily:

'What right have you to search us? But this is Comrade Lenin! Show us your warrants?'

'We do not need any warrants,' barked one man, 'we can do what we want.'

The bandits turned their attention to me and told me to get out. Their order was backed by the threat of their revolvers. It was a shame that armed and strong as I was, I could do nothing but submit. I only knew one thing: not to risk Vladimir Ilyich's life.

One of the attackers climbed into my seat, the others went into the back of the car. The car suddenly dashed forward, obviously driven by an experienced motorist, and disappeared from sight.

'Yah, that was clever', declared Vladimir Ilyich. 'We were armed and yet we gave up the car. Disgraceful!'

I understood that this was aimed at me and began explaining that my shot would have only ended in the robbers opening fire as well.

'But, Vladimir Ilyich, please remember that you were right under the muzzle of their guns. I could have fired, I had enough time, they forgot about me for a minute or two. But what would have been the result? I would have hit one for sure. But after my first shot they would have killed you. I realised this. They were not after us, they only wanted our car.'

On reflection Vladimir Ilyich answered:

'Yes, Comrade Gil, you are right. By using force we would not have gained anything. We escaped with our lives only because we did not oppose them.'

At that moment we noticed that Comrade Chebanov was standing there still clutching a can of milk in his hands (we were taking milk to Krupskaya). Though our situation was far from funny, we all burst out laughing.

I proposed that we should go to the House of the Sokolniki Soviets and phone from there to the Kremlin.

'Is the House of the Soviets really so near?' asked Vladimir Ilyich.

I showed him a two-storey house beyond the bridge. Ilyich spread his arms out in astonishment.

'Robbery right under the nose of the Soviets! That's fantastic.'

We all walked across the bridge. The House of the Soviets, as one would have expected, was all in darkness and the watchman firmly refused to let us in without a pass. Vladimir Ilyich tried to persuade him that we could safely be let in.

'I cannot prove my identity because all my documents were taken away. We were robbed, our car was stolen a few yards from here. We only want to phone to find some means of continuing our trip.'

But the watchman remained stubborn. Vladimir Ilyich was begining to lose patience.

'I am – Lenin,' he said resolutely, 'but I cannot prove it. Here is my driver. He has got his documents and he will testify who I am.'

The watchman was flabbergasted. He turned the lock in the door and stood petrified. I showed him my papers, which he mechanically touched with his fingers, glanced several times at Vladimir Ilyich and without a word let us pass.

There was nobody in the office. I went through several empty rooms and found a dozing telephonist. I asked him to phone the head of the office or his deputy. Soon the deputy came in and asked:

'Who are you? What can I do for you?'

Vladimir Ilyich introduced himself and said:

'Very good manners. People are robbed in the streets, right under your nose.' Then he added: 'May I please use the phone. I should like to ask for another car.'

'Please, come into the office, Comrade Lenin,' said the official in a greatly agitated voice.

Vladimir Ilyich told me to phone Dzerzhinsky. But I could not get hold of him. I reached his deputy and told him all that had happened. Then I passed the receiver to Vladimir Ilyich, whom I heard giving instructions about another car and expressing his horror at the lack of security in the city. Those at the other end of the line must have been wondering whether the whole affair had a political meaning, since Lenin added:

'No, no, no, certainly not political,' Lenin said categorically, 'if it had been, they would have shot me immediately. It was robbery, pure and simple.'[7]

SALARY: LETTER TO V. D. BONCH-BRUEVICH, OFFICE MANAGER, COUNCIL OF THE PEOPLE'S COMMISSARS

23 May 1918

In view of your failure to fulfil my insistent request to point out to me the justification for raising my salary as from 1 March 1918 from 500 to 800 roubles a month, and in view of the obvious illegality of this increase carried out by you arbitrarily by agreement with the secretary of the Council, N. P. Gorbunov, and in direct infringement of the decree of the Council of the People's Commissars of 23 November 1917, I give you a severe reprimand.

V. Ulyanov (Lenin)

Chairman, Council of the People's Commissars[8]

EXPENSES ON GARAGE: LETTER TO F. G. DZERZHINSKY

19 May 1922

Comrade Dzerzhinsky,

I have a serious apprehension: there seems to be some 'excess' in the expenditure on my garage, which I believe is under the special supervision of the G.P.U. Isn't it time to 'compress' this establishment and reduce the expenditure? Everyone reduces expenditure everywhere.

Please, show this to my 'deputies' Rykov and Tsyurupa, and assign a reliable, intelligent, knowledgeable man to check up on whether the expenses under this head can be decreased and compressed, reduced to the utmost.*

Lenin[9]

* On the note is the following conclusion by F. E. Dzerzhinsky and signed by Tsyurupa and Rykov: 'I consider reduction here inadmissible. The pool has six cars and only twelve men. Wage rates – normal, car maintenance – good. No idle running of cars.'

EXPENSES ON BOOKS:
LETTER TO V. D. BONCH-BRUEVICH

4 January 1920

Dear V.D.,
I am paying personally for my library.
When you are well again, please pay everything:

$$3,200$$
$$+ \quad 500 \quad \text{(Dahl)}$$
$$\overline{}$$
$$3,700, \text{ etc.,}$$

and *keep the receipts*

Yours,

Lenin

I enclose 4,000 roubles.
The library of the P.C.P.'s *Managing Department* is another matter.[10]

'PLEASE PROLONG MY LEAVE':
LETTER TO V. M. MOLOTOV FOR THE
POLITBUREAU OF THE R.C.P.(b)C.C.*

16 December 1921

Comrade Molotov,
Please prolong my leave, according to the doctor's orders, for a period of up to two weeks (depending on the course of treatment).
I shall attend the C.C. plenum on some questions, at any rate.
In accordance with the Politbureau decision, I shall give a short report at the Congress of Soviets.

Lenin

Dictated over the phone.[11]

* Russian Communist Party (bolsheviks) Central Committee.

8 March 1922

Dear Comrade Varga,

I am ill. I am quite *incapable* of undertaking any work at all.

If you compile a collection (of quotations from my works or parts of them) I do not, of course, object to this, but you must state that you are responsible for the selection.

Here is my request:

1) quote as fully as possible my works of the spring of 1918 against the 'Leftists', about 'State capitalism' and the difficulties of *administration*, as a *specific* task;

2) (quote more fully) my pamphlet against 'Infantile Disorder' (general rules of tactics and strategy);

N.B. 3) *never* quote my speeches (their text is always bad, always imprecisely conveyed); quote only my *works*.

Best regards,

Yours,

Lenin

P.S. Nor can I promise an afterword. *You* will declare yourself responsible for the selection of the quotations.[12]

HOW TO BORROW A BOOK:
LETTER TO THE LIBRARY OF THE RUMYANTSEV MUSEUM

1 September 1920

If, according to the rules, reference publications are not issued for home use, could one not get them for an evening, for the night, when the Library is closed. *I will return them by the morning.*

For reference for *one* day:

1. The two *best*, fullest, dictionaries of the *Greek* language, Greek-German, -French, -Russian or -English.

2. The best *philosophical* dictionaries, dictionaries of philosophical terms: the German, I think, is Eisler; the English, I

think, is Baldwin; the French, I think, is Frank (if there is nothing newer); the Russian, the latest you have.

3. A history of Greek philosophy.

a) Zeller, the complete and latest edition.

b) Gomperz (the Vienna philosopher): *Griechische Denker.*[13]

'PLEASE LOOK THROUGH MY PAMPHLET': LETTER TO G. V. CHICHERIN

Beginning of May 1920

Comrade Chicherin,

I would ask you and Fineberg (or if you are too busy, then a comrade of your choice who has an excellent knowledge of the British socialist movement) to look through my pamphlet,* *or the chapter on Britain,* and advise me whether I have made any mistakes or tactless statements. If it is no trouble, I would particularly ask that any corrections be done separately in pencil.

Yours,

Lenin[14]

'EXCUSE ME, COMRADES': LETTER TO W. KOENNEN, A. THALHEIMER AND P. FROEHLICH

16 June 1921

Respected Comrades,

I have received the copy of your letter to the Central Committee of our party. Many thanks. I have answered orally yesterday. I am now taking the opportunity to stress that I am

* *'Left Wing' Communism – an Infantile Disorder.*

decisively withdrawing the rude and unkind words I had used and I insist on repeating in writing what I told you before: please, excuse me.*

With communist greetings,

Lenin[15]

* 'The rude and unkind words' must have been used by Lenin in a discussion of the German delegates to the Third Congress of the Comintern with members of the Politbureau of the Russian party. No record of the discussion apparently exists, but a note has been preserved which says: 'Scolding the left German V.K.P.D.'

III. INESSA ARMAND

first half of May 1914

*. . . and not in 1912, but in 1911) we in the editorial office of *Social-Democrat* received Vinnichenko's pamphlet in Russian devoted to a defence against the accusations levelled at him by the Social-Democrats for 'Honesty to Oneself'. Vinnichenko asked for an answer in writing and in print. I remember being impressed by the pamphlet, and I wanted to write about it, but was prevented by all kinds of petty affairs (oh, those 'petty affairs', those apologies for business, pretence of business, a hindrance to business), how I hate fuss and bustle and petty affairs, and how tied I am to them inseparably and for all time!! That's a sign more that I am lazy and tired and bad-tempered. †Generally I like my profession and now I almost hate it.† By the way, I mislaid that pamphlet (published in Lvov) and have forgotten its title. Find it if you can, read it and send it to me.

I thought Vinnichenko sincere and naïve when he puts the question: 'Does a Social-Democrat have the right (!!*sic*!!) to visit a brothel?' and keeps harping on this question, but all the same *individually*. He is sort of half-anarchist or total anarchist. . . .

He once gave a lecture in Paris on 'Honesty to Oneself' with Lunacharsky in the chair, did he not? Or are things in such a way that Lunacharsky is *for* Vinnichenko, while Alexinsky is against? †I would like to know some more details about it.†

†Before leaving Paris you must† discuss with Nik. Vas., Kamsky and Ludmila the question of the delegation to the Vienna Congress. . . .[1]

before 5 July 1914

I have just read, †my dear friend,† Vinnichenko's new novel which you sent me. There's balderdash and stupidity! To combine together as much as possible of every kind of 'horror',

---

* The beginning of this letter is missing– it is available from page 3 only. Throughout, second person singular is used.

† In this section and elsewhere, the passages between †s are in English in the original.

to collect in one story 'depravity' and 'syphilis' and romantic crime, with extortion of money by means of blackmail (with the sister of the blackmailed person turned into a mistress), and the trial of the doctor! All this with hysterical outbursts, eccentricities, claims of having one's 'own' theory of organising prostitutes. This organisation represents nothing bad in itself; but it is the *author*, Vinnichenko himself, who makes nonsense of it, *smacks his lips* over it, makes it his 'hobby horse'.

The review in *Rech* says that it is an imitation of Dostoevsky and that there are good parts in it. This is an imitation, in my opinion, and a supremely bad imitation of the supremely bad in Dostoevsky. Of course, in real life there are individual cases of all the 'horrors' which Vinnichenko describes. But to lump them all together, and in *such* a way, means laying on the horrors *with a trowel*, frightening both one's own imagination and the reader's, 'stunning' both oneself and the reader.

Once I had to spend a night with a sick comrade (*delirium tremens*), and once I had to 'talk round' a comrade who had attempted suicide (after the attempt), and who some years later did commit suicide. Both recollections *à la* Vinnichenko. But in both cases these were small fragments of the lives of both comrades. But this pretentious, crass idiot Vinnichenko, in self-admiration, has from such things compiled a collection that is nothing but horrors – a kind of 'twopenny dreadful'. Brrr. . . . Muck, nonsense. Pity I spent so much time reading it.

P.S. How are things going with your arrangements for the summer?

Yours,

V.I.

Franchement, continuez vous à vous fâcher ou non ? [this sentence in French][2]

before 6 July 1914

†Dear Friend,†

I am terribly afraid that you will refuse to go to Brussels, and thus place us in an *absolutely impossible* position. And so I have thought up another 'compromise', which you will simply be unable to refuse.

Nadya believes your elder children have arrived already, and you could easily leave them for three days (or take Andrei with you).

In the event of the elder children not having arrived and it being *absolutely* impossible for you to leave the children for three days, I suggest that you go *for one day* (the 16th, *even* for *half a day*, to read the report), either leaving the children for the day or even sending for K-vich for that day as a last resort. (We shall pay expenses.)

You see, it's *extremely* important that the main report at least, should be read *really effectively*. And for that purpose *excellent* French is definitely needed, otherwise the effect will be nil – *French*, because otherwise nine-tenths will be *lost* in translation for the very Executive Committee *for whom the effect is primarily intended* (the Germans are *hopeless*, and they *may* not be there).

Besides excellent French, of course, an *understanding of essentials* and proper tact are needed. You are the *only suitable person*. So please – I beg you most earnestly – consent, if only for one day (you will read the report and apologise, pleading illness in the family, and go away, handing things over to Popov). If you have already refused by letter, wire (Ulyanov. Poronin – ten words cost sixty heller): 'agree one day', 'agree sixteenth only', etc.

A strong handshake. Sincerely devoted to you.

V.I.

We shall write the report of the C.C. Your job will be to translate and read it *with commentaries* on which we shall agree.

P.S. †The new chairman is not here but must come very soon. ... I hope you will not now decline my demand. A good 'lecture' in French, in good French will help our party extremely.†

I am very worried about Brussels. *Only you* could carry it off wonderfully. . . .[3]

before 13 July 1914

Dear Friend,

I am extremely grateful to you for agreeing. I am absolutely sure you'll carry off your important role with flying colours and give a fitting answer to Plekhanov, Rosa Luxemburg, and Rubanovich (the insolent fellow) who are going to Brussels in the hope of staging a demonstration against us generally and against me in particular.

You are sufficiently familiar with the business, you speak well, I am sure you now have enough 'cheek'. Please, do not take my occasional advice amiss. It is meant to facilitate your difficult task. Plekhanov likes to 'disconcert' women comrades with sudden gallantries (in French, and so on). You must be prepared to meet this with a quick repartee – 'I am delighted, Comrade Plekhanov, you are quite an old spark' (or a gallant cavalier) – or something like that in order, politely, to put him in his place. You should know that everybody will be very angry (I'm very glad!) at my not being present, and will probably want to take it out on you. But I am sure you will show them your 'claws' in the best possible way. I am tickled in advance at the thought of the cool, calm and somewhat scornful snub they will be publicly inviting.

Plekhanov likes to heckle and bully his victim. My advice is – cut him short immediately, saying: 'you have a right, as has every member of this conference, to ask questions, but I am not answering you personally, I am answering the whole conference, so will you please not interrupt me' – and by this means, promptly turn his heckling into an *attack* upon him. You should be on the offensive all the time. Or, say: I shall *take the floor* when my turn comes, in lieu of an answer and for an answer (I prefer it *that way*), and you will be quite satisfied. In my experience this is the best way to deal with insolent fellows. They are cowards and will sing low at once.

They don't like it when we quote resolutions. But that is the best answer: I have come here chiefly to convey the *officially documented* decisions of our workers' party. For those who are interested in these decisions I shall explain one of them.

... I advise you not to forget the *official* definition of the aim of the conference.

To exchange opinions
on moot points!

Just that! To explain opinions – that is what you are doing.
Another important subject for *popular* elucidation (you have
to be extra-popular with the French) is that of the illegal
organisation, of the complete trust, secrecy, etc., which it calls
for. It is all very well for you Europeans: you have open control
and verification. Everything is easy then.

With us, however, an open and accurate record of party
membership in an illegal organisation is impossible, as is also
open control. Therefore the maximum trust is needed in order
to maintain discipline and good teamwork, whereas the 'liquidators', in rejecting the idea of an underground, are destroying
the very possibility of joint work. . . .[4]

19 July 1914

Huysmans and Vandervelde have unleashed *all* threats.
Wretched diplomats! They thought they could frighten us (or
you). Of course, they have failed.

. . . . You handled the matter better than I could have done.
Language apart, I would certainly have *blown my top*. I would
not have been able to stand the hypocrisy and would have called
them scoundrels. *And that's what they were waiting for* – that's
what they were trying to provoke.

The others and you carried it off calmly and firmly. †Extre-
mely thankful and greetings to you. . . .†

Awaiting your impressions,

Yours,

V.U.[5]

---

* Second person singular is used throughout.

19 July 1914

†My dear and dearest friend,
  Today for the first time I have a good report (very, very good!) – obviously written by Kamski. I greet you a thousand times!! Your task was heavy and . . . Huysmans had done all against you and our delegation, but your have *dejoué* his sallies in the best manner. You have rendered a very great service to our party! I am especially thankful because you have replaced me. . . .[6]†

after 4 June 1915

Dear Friend†
  I have already written to you twice but here, to tell the truth, there is little that is new. From Russia news is not bad, but this, I hope, you'll soon read yourself when you come. Why don't you write anything about the date of your dental treatment? At least approximately? One has to travel either by post coach (to Flühli – twice daily, at 9 a.m. and at 4 p.m. from Schüpfheim, and to us, to Sörenberg, only once daily, at 9 a.m. from Schüpfheim. To catch the morning coach one has, *I think*, to leave Berne at 5.30 *in the morning* and wait one hour and a half at Schüpfheim. If one leaves Berne at 2.05, as we did, the post coach that one catches goes only to Flühli; further one has to hire horses (to do this one has to *telephone* from Schüpfheim – there is a restaurant opposite the station. The owner, for 10 pfg would phone us here, Hotel Marienthal in Sörenberg, and say that you are coming *to me* and that a horse carriage should be sent; in this way they will manage to fetch you from Flühli and bring you here).
  The post coach costs 1fr. 20 to Flühli + 2 frs from Flühli to Sörenberg.
  A horse from here costs 4 frs per person (6 frs for two) from Flühli to Sörenberg.
  Your letter for some reason went to Lucerne! I do not under-

stand why. Perhaps because you did not write Sörenberg on a new line? Or did not add *via Schüpfheim?*

A handshake,

Yours,

Lenin

P.S. . . . One more request (oh-oh! you'll get quite crushed under the load of things and requests, won't you?); buy some lemon crystals (*Zitronensäure*). It's bad to go for a holiday later than others!

From Neuchâtel *still no answer.** Very odd!! *Au revoir. . . .*[7]

later than 4 June 1915

†*Dear Friend!*

I am astonished that we have had no news from you for many days. I hope it is because you will come soon.† One more request – if you are very fed up with all requests (I feel a pang of remorse, because you had already quite a lot of them), don't bother, I can write from here – but if you pass by Kaiser's, ask for a *sample* of large envelopes (the size of the enclosed sheet or folded flat in two, in width) for sending thick manuscripts. Buy a few dozen: *thirty.* In this shop there are samples of all sorts of envelopes (I need *strong* ones, the cheapest but strong) with the price list for 10, 50, 100 envelopes.

Here it keeps on raining. I hope the heavenly office will have poured out all the surplus water before you come and then the weather will be good. Did you get yourself some good French novels from the library (Stadtbibliothek)? I have read here *Les Châtiments* of V. Hugo, and liked it as before. I am cross that from the Neuchâtel library there is still no answer!!

Au revoir

Yours,

Lenin

* From the library to which Lenin applied for a book to be sent to Sörenberg.

One more request: in case we should go for *long* excursions with you (this is not certain, but we may manage sometimes), it would be worth knowing what are the conditions in the *Hütten* (*cabanes*) – the huts with beds in the mountains set up by the Swiss 'Alpine' club. Pop into the office of this club in Berne (I do not know the address: in *Verkehrsbureau* – *bureau de renseignements* they will tell you) get the prospectuses and ask for details. I often study the *Baedeker* and 'look attentively at' such *cabanes* at the height of 2,500 – 3,000 m not far from us.

Why don't you write what the dentist told you? When do you come?

If you go to the *Stadtbibliothek*, look through the catalogues more thoroughly. About French classics, poets and prose writers.

P.S. The information from the Swiss Alpine Club:

1. What is the cost of the 'huts' for non-members.

2. Are there any *collective* climbing expeditions to high peaks (3,000 – 3,500 m), and how and when, etc.[8]

13 January 1916

Dear Friend,

Not a scrap of news from you. We do not know how you have arrived and how you are. Did you manage to settle down well? Is the work in the library going well? We have received a letter addressed to you from a prisoner of war. The letter was delivered to another Russian (are you sure you have not given the wrong address – our address? You did not forget to put the correct number?). . . .

A firm handshake and best wishes of success in your work.

Yours,

Ivan[9]

15 January 1916

Dear Friend,

... Today is a beautiful sunny day with light snow. For the first time after the 'flu we went with my wife for a walk to *Frauen-Kapelle*, along the same road – do you remember? – along which we had such a wonderful walk, the three of us. I kept on recalling it and regretted you were not with us.

Incidentally, I am a bit surprised that there is no news from you. I have to confess one thing: it occurred to me – sinfully – were you 'offended' by any chance because I failed to see you off on the day of your departure? I repent, I repent and reject such thoughts and have already pushed them away.

This is my second postcard. Has the first one got lost? I am repeating some important advice: read nrs 5 and 6 of *Nashe Slovo* once more and once more!! Kollontay writes *good* stuff from America, *publishes Internationale Flugblätter*. From Russia also *good* news.

A firm handshake,

Yours,

Lenin[10]

19 January 1916

Dear Friend

I am sending you the third postcard already. This time in French so as to ease the task of the censors in case they cause delay in the delivery of letters. To tell the truth, I have been anxious for the last few days: no news from you whatsoever! If you were cross with me, then you would probably have written to other friends, but, as far as I know, you have not written to anybody. If within the next few days I do not get a letter from you, I shall write to our friends to find out whether you are ill. I have already inquired several times whether there were any *poste restante* letters – there was nothing. ...

I wrote to 'your' editor in one of the towns of Italian Switzerland. He does not answer at all. It's strange, isn't it? We are all waiting impatiently for you to make arrangements about literary work and novels in Paris, where you'll certainly find many people, writers, publishers and so on, as you are working in the National Library and are well acquainted with these people.

The weather is fine. Last Sunday we went for a lovely walk to 'our' little mountain. The view over the Alps was particularly beautiful; I very much regretted you were not with us.

A few days ago Camille Huysmans made a very big and 'diplomatic' speech at the Congress of the Dutch party. I do not know whether you'll find the text in the French papers. If not, you'll find it here. . . .

How are you getting on? Are you content? Don't you feel lonely? Are you very busy? You are causing me great anxiety by not giving me any news about yourself! . . . Where do you live? Where do you eat? At the 'buffet' of the National Library?

I am asking you once more for letters *poste restante*.

Devotedly yours,

Your *Basil*

P.S. Again nothing! No letters from you.[11]

21 January 1916

Dear Friend,

Only today we received your long letter, which gave us great pleasure. This is my fourth letter to you: all the previous three postcards were sent *poste restante*. If you have not received them, it means that either they get lost or there are some special rules (or misrules) in regard to *poste restante* mail. . . .

Yes, I nearly forgot (I am in a hurry to get this off by the next train). If there are special misrules about *poste restante* letters then maybe this is the reason I am not getting any letters (I have not had a *single one* from you) although you do write? Drop a line quickly: if you underline the date twice, that means you *receive* my letters and *you write to me*. Drop a line on the address at which we received your long letter.

Firm handshake,

Yours,

Lenin

Why did you not give your address before?[12]

20 November 1916

Dear Friend,

Of course, I also want to correspond. Let's continue our correspondence.

How I laughed over your postcard, I really had to hold my sides, as they say. 'In France there is no such measure as the hectare but there is the acre, and you don't know how big an acre is. . . .'

That really is funny!

It was *France – imaginez-vous?* – that introduced the metric system, adopted in most countries of the world, a ha = hectare = 100 ares. An acre is *not* a French measure, but an English one, about 4/10 of a hectare.

You mustn't be offended by my laughter. I didn't mean any harm. After all, is it so surprising that you do not often come across the words hectare, ha, etc.? They are dull, technical words.

Many thanks for translating the theses. . . .

'The working man has no country' – this means that (a) his economic position (*le salariat*) is not national but international, (b) his class enemy is international, (c) the conditions of his emancipation also, (d) the international unity of the workers is *more important* than the national.

Does this mean, does it follow from this, that we *should not* fight when it is a question of throwing off a foreign yoke?? Yes or no?

A war of colonies for emancipation?

– or Ireland against England?

And an insurrection (national), is not that defence of the fatherland? ...

If you need more books, *write*. One can get a lot here, and anyhow I am often in the libraries.

All the best.

Lenin[13]

25 November 1916

Dear Friend,

... As regards the fatherland, you evidently want to establish a contradiction between my previous writings (when? 1913? where precisely? what precisely?) and the present ones. I do not think there are any contradictions. Find the exact texts, then we shall look at it again. ...

That the defence of the fatherland is admissible (when it is admissible) only as the defence of democracy (in the appropriate epoch), is my opinion too.

Of course, the proletariat should never 'merge' with the general democratic movement. Marx and Engels did not 'merge' with the bourgeois-democratic movement in Germany in 1848. We Bolsheviks did not 'merge' with the bourgeois-democratic movement in 1905.

We Social-Democrats always stand for democracy, not 'in the name of capitalism', but in the name of clearing the path for *our* movement, which clearing is impossible without the development of capitalism.

Best greetings,

Yours,

Lenin

P.S. If you need books, write.[14]

30 November 1916

Dear Friend,

As regards 'defence of the fatherland' I don't know whether we differ or not. You find a contradiction between my article in the collection of articles *To the Memory of Marx* and my present statements, *without quoting* either precisely. I cannot reply to this. I haven't got the collection *To the Memory of Marx.* Of course, I cannot remember word for word what I wrote in it. Without *precise* quotations, then and now, I am not able to reply to *such* an argument on your part.

But *generally* speaking, it seems to me that you argue somehow in a somewhat one-sided and formalistic manner. You have taken *one* quotation from the *Communist Manifesto* ('the working man has no country') and you seem to want to apply it without any reservations, *up to and including the repudiation of national wars.*

The whole spirit of Marxism, its whole system, demands that each proposition should be considered (a) only historically, (b) only in connection with others, (c) only in connection with the concrete experience of history.

The fatherland is a historical concept. The fatherland in an epoch or, more precisely, at the *moment* of struggle for the overthrow of national oppression, is one thing. At the moment when national movements have been left far behind, it is another thing. For the 'three types of countries' (paragraph 6 of our theses on self-determination) there *cannot be* a proposition about the fatherland and its defence identically applicable in all conditions.

In the *Communist Manifesto* it is said that the working men have no country.

Correct. But *not only* this is stated there. It is stated there also that when national states are being formed, the role of the proletariat is somewhat special. To take the first proposition (the working man has no country) and *forget* its *connection* with the second (the workers are constituted as a class nationally, though not in the same sense as the bourgeoisie) will be exceptionally incorrect.

Where, then, does the connection lie? In my opinion precisely in the fact that in the *democratic* movement (at such a moment, in such concrete circumstances) the proletariat cannot refuse to support it (and, consequently, support defence of the fatherland in a national war).

Marx and Engels said in the *Communist Manifesto* that the

working man has no country. But the same Marx *called* for a *national* war more than once: Marx in 1848, Engels in 1859 (the end of his pamphlet *Po and Rhine*, where the *national* feeling of the Germans is directly inflamed, where they are directly called upon to wage a national *war*). Engels in 1891, in view of the then threatening and advancing war of France (Boulanger) + Alexander III against Germany, directly recognised 'defence of the fatherland'.

Were Marx and Engels muddlers who said one thing today and another thing tomorrow? No. In my view, admission of 'defence of the fatherland' in a national war *fully* answers the requirements of Marxism. In 1891 the German *Social-Democrats* really *should have* defended their fatherland in a war against Boulanger + Alexander III. This would have been a peculiar variety of *national* war. . . .[15]

18 December 1916

Dear Friend,

. . . I have been reading the *Plaidoirie* [*Guerre à la Guerre*] by Humbert-Droz. My God, what a philistine of Tolstoyism!! I have written again to Abramovich. Is he really hopeless after all? I am wondering whether there are not in Switzerland bacilli of petty-bourgeois (and petty-state) thick-wittedness, Tolstoyism, and pacifism, which destroy the best people? I am sure there must be! . . .

P.S. Do you ski? You really should! Learn the knack, get yourself skis and go off to the mountains – you must. It's good in the mountains in winter! It is delightful, and smells of Russia.[16]

after 23 December 1916

Dear Friend,

. . . As regards defence of the fatherland. It would be most unpleasant for me if we differed on this. Let us try once more to come to an agreement.

Here is some 'material for reflection':

War is the continuation of politics.

Everything depends on the system of political relations before the war and during the war.

The main types of these systems are (a) the relation of the oppressed nation to the oppressing, (b) the relation between two oppressing nations on account of the loot, its division, etc., (c) the relation of a national state which does not oppress others to one which oppresses, to a particularly reactionary state.

Think this over.

Caesarism in France + tsarism in Russia against the *non-imperialist* Germany in 1891 – that was the historical situation in 1891.

Think that over! And I was writing of *1891* in no. 1 of *Sbornik* as well. . . .

Yours,

Lenin[17]

13 December 1916

Dear Friend,

. . . A war of France + Russia against Germany in 1891. You take 'my criterion' and apply it *only* to France and Russia!!! For pity's sake, where is the logic here? That's just what I say, that *on the part of France and Russia* it would have been a reactionary war (a war in order to turn back the development of Germany, to return her from national unity to dismemberment). *But on the part of Germany?* You are silent. Yet that is the chief thing. For Germany in 1891 the war did not and could not have an imperialist character.

You have forgotten the main thing – that in 1891 no imperialism existed at all (I have tried to show in my pamphlet that it was born in 1898–1900, not earlier), and there was no imperialist war, there could not be, on the part of Germany. (By the way, there was no revolutionary Russia then either: that is very important.)

Furthermore, you write: 'The "possibility" of the dismemberment of Germany is not excluded in the 1914–17 war either', simply sliding away from the assessment of what exists to what is *possible*.

That is not historical. It is not political.

What *exists* today is an *imperialist* war on *both* sides. This we have said a thousand times. This is the essence.

And the 'possible'? All kinds of things are 'possible'. It is ridiculous to deny the '*possibility*' of transforming the imperialist war into a national war. . . . What is not 'possible' in this world? But *so far* it has not been transformed. Marxism postulates its policy on the basis of the *actual*, not the 'possible'. It is possible that one phenomenon will change into another – and our tactics are not ossified. *Parlez-moi de la réalité et non pas des possibilités*!

Engels was right. In my time I have heard an awful lot of hasty charges that Engels was an opportunist, and my attitude is supremely distrustful. Try, I say, and prove first that Engels was wrong. You won't prove it! . . .

No. No. Engels was *not* infallible. Marx was *not* infallible. But if you want to point out their 'fallibility' you have to set about it differently, really, quite differently. Otherwise you are a thousand times wrong.

A firm, firm handshake,

Yours,

Lenin[18]

13 January 1917

. . . I wish you all the very best, and ask you again to make a trip somewhere, if only for a time, if only with lectures or anything else, so as to have a change, to throw yourself into some absorbing occupation, something useful to new and fresh people. Believe me, work among the French is much needed and extremely useful. . . .[19]

14 January 1917

Dear Friend,

I know how terribly bad you feel and I am eagerly anxious to help you in any way I can. What about you trying to live at some place where there are friends and where you could regularly have talks on party affairs and regularly take part in them ? . . .[20]

15 January 1917

. . . I trust that you are not answering my suggestion about your French lecture trip not because you are absolutely against it, but simply because you are considering this plan with the idea of accepting it. I am not hurrying you, and shall not repeat my persuasions but I would very much like you to take a change of air, to visit new and old friends. I would dearly love to say a lot of kind words to you and to make things easier for you until you get into your stride with work that will engross you completely.

All the very best,

Yours,

Lenin[21]

16 January 1917

Dear Friend,

If Switzerland is drawn into the war, the French will occupy Geneva immediately. To be in Geneva then is to be in France, and from there, to be in touch with Russia. I am therefore thinking of turning over the *party* funds to you (for you to keep *on your person*, sewed up in a special little bag, as the bank won't let you draw it during the war). I am writing to Grigory

[Zinoviev] about this. These are merely plans, between ourselves for the time being.

I think that we shall remain in Zurich, that war is improbable.

My very best regards,

Yours,

Lenin[22]

19 January 1917

Dear Friend,

About Engels. If you have come across the issue of *Neue Zeit* with Kautsky's story (and Engels's letters) about how they distorted Engel's preface to *Klassenkämpfe*, it would be a good thing if you copied it out in full in a special notebook. If you can't, then send me the exact number of *Neue Zeit*, the year, volume and page.

Your attacks on Engels, I am convinced, are totally groundless. Excuse my frankness: one must prepare oneself much more seriously before writing like that! Otherwise it is easy to disgrace oneself – I warn you *entre nous*, as a friend, between ourselves, in case you begin talking *in this way* one day in the press or at a meeting. . . .

Best greetings and wishes,

Yours,

Lenin[23]

between 25 and 31 March 1917

Dear Friend,

You must be in an excessively nervous state. This is my explanation for a number of theoretical 'oddities' in your letters.

One should not make a distinction between the first and the second revolution, or the first and the second stage ? ?

That's just what one must do. Marxism requires us to distinguish which *classes* are in action. In Russia *not the same* class than before is in power. That means that the revolution which lies ahead is quite, quite *different*.

My phrase about the support of the workers by the Miliukovs has (it seemed to me) a clear meaning: *if* the Miliukovs really wanted to finish off the monarchy, they *should have* supported the workers. Only that!

One must not make a 'fetish' of revolution. Kerensky is a revolutionary but also a chatterbox, a petty liar, a deceiver of workers. It is almost certain that *even* in the Petrograd 'Soviet of Workers' and Soldiers' Deputies' the *majority* has been fooled by him (with the help of the wobbling and muddling Chkheidze). And what will happen to the countryside?

It is *quite* possible that *for a time* the majority both of the workers and of the peasants will really be *for* the imperialist war. . . .

It would be a good thing if someone with free time (better still a group, but if one does not exist, then at least an individual) undertook *to collect all* the telegrams (and articles if possible) in *all* the foreign newspapers about the Russian revolution.

There are mountains of material. It is impossible to follow it all.

Probably we *won't* manage to get to Russia!! Britain *will not let us through*. It can't be done through Germany.

Greetings!

Lenin[24]

March 1920

Dear Friend,

So, the doctor says [you have] pneumonia
You have to be *extra*-careful.
You must make your daughter phone me every day (12–4).
Write *frankly,* what do you need?
Do you *have* wood? Who makes the fire?
Do you have food? Who prepares it?
Who makes you compresses (fomentation)?

You are evading the questions – that's not good. Answer straightway on the same sheet, answer *ALL* MY POINTS
Get well!

Your Lenin

Is the telephone repaired ?[25]

ANGELICA BALABANOFF

DEATH AND FUNERAL

I saw Lenin at the funeral of someone particularly dear to him.
I never saw such torment; I never saw any human being so
completely absorbed by sorrow, by the effort to keep it to himself, to guard it against the attention of others, as if their awareness could have diminished the intensity of his feeling. . . .

Because of her indefatigable work and great privations, her
physical condition had been such that the Bolshevik Central
Committee sent her to the Caucasus for a rest period. Her
weakened body could not withstand the epidemic that had
broken out there, aided by the local unhygienic conditions. She
died of typhus fever in 1920. Her body was transferred to
Moscow for burial. . . .

At that time one had to fear attempts on the lives of the most
prominent communists. One of the precautionary measures
was a chain of the most trusted workers, who, by holding hands,
would form a circle around us. Thus, I found myself in the
immediate vicinity of Lenin. Not only his face but his whole
body expressed so much sorrow that I dared not greet him, not
even with the slightest gesture. It was clear he wanted to be
alone with his grief. He seemed to have shrunk; his cap almost
covered his face, his eyes seemed drowned in tears held back
with effort. As our circle moved, following the movement of the
people, he too moved, without offering resistance, as if he were
grateful for being brought nearer to his dead comrade. This
mood did not influence in the least his activity as statesman and
strategist of the workers' movement of the world. From the
funeral he went straight back to his desk.[26]

ALEXANDRA KOLLONTAY REMEMBERS

... We talked often about Lenin and, of course, about the causes which provoked his death at the age of 54. One day she [Kollontay] said:

'He could not survive Inessa Armand. Inessa's death hastened the development of the sickness which was undermining his life. . . .'

'Inessa? . . .

'Yes, when in 1921 her body was brought from the Caucasus (where she died of typhus) and we were all following the hearse to the cemetery, Lenin was unrecognisable. He walked with his eyes closed and we thought that at any moment he would faint. . . .'

'Where did he meet her?'

'In Paris. Nadezhda Konstantinovna knew about it. She knew that Lenin was greatly attached to Inessa and several times she proposed that she would leave. Lenin, however, told her: "No, stay . . .".'

'At the women's congresses', added Kollontay, 'Inessa's "theses" were always carried. A few of us knew that it was Lenin who prepared them.'

I knew that Inessa played an important role in the women's movement and that she used to see Lenin. I used to meet her in 1919, during the period when intrigues provoked a split among the Frenchmen in Moscow who had rallied to the revolution. I kept her *au courant* on the state of affairs, even asking her to pass the information to Lenin.[27]

IV. REVOLUTION, LITERATURE AND ART

WHAT IS TO BE DONE?

1901-2

... 'We should dream!' I wrote these words and became
alarmed. I imagined myself sitting at a 'unity conference' and
opposite me were the *Rabocheye Delo* editors and contributors.
Comrade Martynov rises and, turning to me, says sternly:
'Permit me to ask you: has an autonomous editorial board the
right to dream without first soliciting the opinion of the party
committees?' He is followed by Comrade Krichevsky, who
(philosophically deepening Comrade Martynov, who long ago
rendered Comrade Plekhanov more profound) continues more
sternly: 'I go further. I ask: has a Marxist any right at
all to dream, knowing that according to Marx mankind always
sets itself the tasks it can solve and that tactics is a process
of the growth of party tasks which grow together with the
party?'

The very thought of these stern questions sends a cold shiver
down my spine and makes me wish for nothing but a place to
hide in. I shall try to hide behind the back of Pisarev.

'There are rifts and rifts', wrote Pisarev of the rift between
dreams and reality. 'My dream may run ahead of the natural
march of events or may go off at a tangent in a direction in which
no natural march of events will ever proceed. In the first case my
dream will not cause any harm; it may even support and increase
the energy of the working man. . . . There is nothing in such
dreams that would distort or paralyse working power. On the
contrary, if man were completely deprived of the ability to
dream in this way, if he could not from time to time run ahead
and mentally conceive, in an entire and complete picture, the
product to which his hands are only just beginning to lend shape,
then I cannot at all imagine what stimulus there would be to
induce man to undertake and complete extensive and strenuous
work in the sphere of art, science, and practical endeavour. . . .
The rift between dreams and reality causes no harm only if the
person dreaming believes seriously in his dream, if he attentively observes life, compares his observations with his castles

in the air, and if, generally speaking, he works conscientiously for the achievement of his fantasies. If there is some connection between dreams and life then all is well.'

Of this kind of dreaming there is unfortunately too little in our movement. . . .[1]

FINE PAGES OF RUSSIAN LITERATURE

'Vladimir Ilyich', [said Olminsky], 'surely you must be sickened by what Samsonov is saying! Listen to the landlord's son giving himself away! The truth will out: here he is, gibbering about his country estate. He talks about flowers and the way they smell just like a 16-year-old schoolgirl. Just see how carried away he is when he talks about the beauty of the lime and birch trees. A revolutionary has no right to forget that landowners used to flog their peasants and house-serfs with birch-rods in those beautiful lime-tree avenues. I can see from Samsonov's tale how much he would like to return to the scene of his happy childhood. Surrender to such feelings is dangerous for a revolutionary. You begin to pine, and soon you feel like buying yourself a little estate. Then before long you'll find yourself wanting the peasants to get on with the work while you lie in a hammock with a French novel in your hand and doze comfortably in your lime-tree avenue.'

Lenin . . . stuck his thumbs into the armholes of his waistcoat, and began to deliver a retort. . . . He spoke sharply, with unconcealed irritation.

'Well, Mikhail Stepanovich [Olminsky], you surprise me! To listen to you, it would seem that many fine pages of Russian literature ought to be considered harmful, and, for all I know, torn out and burned. What you say strikes at the best pages of Turgenev, Tolstoy, Aksakov. Up till now the landowning nobility has made the chief contribution to our literature. Their financial position and their way of life (which included lime-tree avenues and flowerbeds, too) made it possible for them to create works of art which are a source of delight – and not only to us Russians. You say there can be no charm in the old lime-tree avenues because they were planted by the hands of serfs, or because peasants were birched in them. This is the sort of over-simplification that plagued Populism. We Marxists have got over it, thank goodness. If you were right, we should have to turn our backs on the beauty of the temples of antiquity, as well. These temples were created thanks to the barbarous and brutal exploitation of slaves. The high civilisation of antiquity ... was developed entirely on the basis of slavery. I can see absolutely nothing in Samsonov's feelings and words to make you so angry. The man has read Herzen and was carried away by something that reminded him of the place where he was born – and it has made him so homesick for Russia that he would like to get out of this wretched Geneva as fast as he can. What is there so wicked, mysterious or strange in that ? Nothing at all. It's your thinking that's odd, not his. Because Samsonov likes lime-tree and birch-tree avenues and the flowerbeds of country estates, you decide that he must be infected by some specifically feudal psychology, and that he is sure to end up by exploiting peasants. Well, what about me, if it comes to that ? I too used to live on a country estate which belonged to my grand-father. In a sense, I too am a scion of the landed gentry. This is all many years ago, but I still haven't forgotten the pleasant aspects of life on our estate. I have forgotten neither its lime-trees nor its flowers. So go on, put me to death. I remember with pleasure how I used to loll about in haystacks, although I had not made them, how I used to eat strawberries and raspberries, although I had not planted them, and how I used to drink fresh milk, although I had not milked the cows. I gather from what you've just said about Samsonov that you consider such memories unworthy of a revolutionary ? Think it over carefully, Mikhail Stepanovich, aren't you going a bit too far ?'[2]

V. I. LENIN

IN MEMORY OF HERZEN

1912

One hundred years have elapsed since Herzen's birth. The whole of liberal Russia is paying homage to him, studiously evading, however, the serious question of socialism, and taking pains to conceal that which distinguished Herzen the *revolutionary* from a liberal. The right-wing press, too, is commemorating the Herzen centenary, falsely asserting that in his last years Herzen renounced revolution. And in the orations on Herzen that are made by the liberals and Narodniks abroad, phrasemongering reigns supreme. The working-class party should commemorate the Herzen centenary, not for the sake of philistine glorification, but for the purpose of making clear its own tasks and ascertaining the place actually held in history by this writer who played a great part in paving the way for the Russian revolution.

Herzen belonged to the generation of revolutionaries among the nobility and landlords of the first half of the last century. The nobility gave Russia the Birons and Arakcheyevs, innumerable 'drunken' roisterers, floggers, pimps, as well as amiable Manilovs.* 'But', wrote Herzen, 'among them developed the men of 14 December,‡ a phalanx of heroes reared, like Romulus and Remus, on the milk of a wild beast. . . . They were veritable Titans, hammered out of pure steel from head to foot, comrades-in-arms who deliberately went to certain death in order to awaken the young generation to a new life and to purify the children born in an environment of tyranny and servility.'

Herzen was one of those children. The uprising of the Decembrists awakened and 'purified' him. In the feudal Russia of the forties of the nineteenth century, he rose to a height which placed him on a level with the greatest thinkers of his time. He assimilated Hegel's dialectics. He realised that it was 'the algebra of the revolution'. He went further than Hegel,

---

* Manilov was a sentimental landowner in Gogol's *Dead Souls*.
‡ Revolutionary noblemen of 1825, the Decembrists.

following Feuerbach to materialism. The first of his *Letters on the Study of Nature*, 'Empiricism and Idealism', written in 1844, reveals to us a thinker who even now stands head and shoulders above the multitude of modern empiricist natural scientists and the host of present-day idealist and semi-idealist philosophers. Herzen came right up to dialectical materialism, and halted – before historical materialism.

It was this 'halt' that caused Herzen's spiritual shipwreck after the defeat of the revolution of 1848. Herzen left Russia, and observed this revolution at close range. He was at that time a democrat, a revolutionary, a socialist. But his 'socialism' was one of the countless forms and varieties of bourgeois and petty-bourgeois socialism of the period of 1848, which was dealt its death-blow in the June days of that year. In point of fact, it was not socialism at all, but so many sentimental phrases, bene-volent visions, which were the expression *at that time* of the revolutionary character of the bourgeois democrats, as well as of the proletariat, which had not yet freed itself from the influence of those democrats.

Herzen's spiritual shipwreck, his deep scepticism and pessimism after 1848, was a shipwreck of the *bourgeois illusions* of socialism. Herzen's spiritual drama was a product and a reflection of that epoch in world history when the revolutionary character of the bourgeois democrats was *already* passing away (in Europe), while the revolutionary character of the socialist proletariat had *not yet* matured. This is something the Russian knights of liberal verbiage, who are now covering up their counter-revolutionary nature by florid phrases about Herzen's scepticism, did not and could not understand. With these knights, who betrayed the Russian revolution of 1905, and have even forgotten to think of the great name of *revolutionary*, scepticism is a form of transition from democracy to liberalism, to that toadying, vile, foul and brutal liberalism which shot down the workers in 1848, restored the shattered thrones and applauded Napoleon III, and which Herzen cursed, unable to understand its class nature.

With Herzen, scepticism was a form of transition from the illusion of a bourgeois democracy that is 'above classes' to the grim, inexorable and invincible class struggle of the proletariat.

The proof: the *Letters to an Old Comrade* – to Bakunin – written by Herzen in 1869, a year before his death. In them Herzen breaks with the anarchist Bakunin. True, Herzen still sees this break as a mere disagreement on tactics and not as a gulf between the world outlook of the proletarian who is confident of the victory of his class and that of the petty bourgeois who has despaired of his salvation. True enough, in these letters as well, Herzen repeats the old bourgeois-democratic phrases to the effect that socialism must preach 'a sermon addressed equally to workman and master, to farmer and townsman'. Nevertheless, in breaking with Bakunin, Herzen turned his gaze, not to liberalism, but to the *International* – to the International led by Marx, to the International which had begun to '*rally the legions*' of the proletariat, to unite '*the world of labour*' which is 'abandoning the world of those who enjoy without working'.

Failing as he did to understand the bourgeois-democratic character of the entire movement of 1848 and of all the forms of pre-Marxist socialism, Herzen was still less able to understand the bourgeois nature of the Russian revolution. Herzen is the founder of 'Russian' socialism, of 'Narodnism'. He saw 'socialism' in the emancipation of the peasants *with land*, in community land tenure and in the peasant idea of 'the right to land'. He set forth his pet ideas on this subject an untold number of times.

Actually, there is *not a grain* of socialism in this doctrine of Herzen's, as, indeed, in the whole of Russian Narodnism, including the faded Narodnism of the present-day Socialist-Revolutionaries. Like the various forms of 'the socialism of 1848' in the West, this is the same sort of sentimental phrases, of benevolent visions, in which is expressed the *revolutionism* of the bourgeois peasant democracy in Russia. The more land the peasants would have received in 1861 and the less they would have to pay for it, the more would the power of the feudal landlords have been undermined and the more rapidly, freely and widely would capitalism have developed in Russia. The idea of the 'right to land' and of 'equalised division of the land', is nothing but a formulation of the revolutionary aspiration for equality cherished by the peasants who are fighting for the complete overthrow of the power of the landlords, for the complete abolition of landlordism.

This was fully proved by the revolution of 1905: on the one hand, the proletariat came out quite independently at the head of the revolutionary struggle, having founded the Social-Democratic Labour Party; on the other hand, the revolutionary peasants, who fought for every form of the abolition of landlordism even to 'the abolition of private landownership', fought precisely as proprietors, as small entrepreneurs. Today, the controversy over the 'socialist nature' of the right to land, and so on, serves only to *obscure* and cover up the really important and serious historical question concerning the difference of *interests* of the liberal bourgeoisie and the revolutionary peasantry in the Russian bourgeois revolution; in other words, the question of the liberal and the democratic, the 'compromising' (monarchist) and the republican trends manifested in that revolution. This is exactly the question posed by Herzen's *Kolokol*, if we turn our attention to the essence of the matter and not to the words, if we investigate the class struggle as the basis of 'theories' and doctrines and not vice versa.

Herzen founded a free Russian press abroad, and that is the great service rendered by him. *Polyarnaya Zvezda* took up the tradition of the Decembrists. *Kolokol* (1857–67) championed the emancipation of the peasants with might and main. The slavish silence was broken.

But Herzen came from a landlord, aristocratic milieu. He had left Russia in 1847, he had not seen the revolutionary people and could have no faith in it. Hence his liberal appeal to the 'upper ranks'. Hence his innumerable sugary letters in *Kolokol* addressed to Alexander II the Hangman, which today one cannot read without revulsion. Chernyshevsky, Dobrolyubov and Serno-Solotyevich, who represented the new generation of revolutionary *raznochintsi*,* were a thousand times right when they reproached Herzen for these departures from democracy to liberalism. However, it must be said in fairness to Herzen that, much as he vacillated between democracy and liberalism,

* *Raznochintsi* – educated children of artisans, merchants, clergy or peasants as distinct from those coming from families of the nobility.

the democrat in him gained the upper hand nonetheless.

When Kavelin, one of the most repulsive exponents of liberal servility – who at one time was enthusiastic about *Kolokol* precisely because of its *liberal* tendencies – rose in arms against 'violence' and appeals for it, and began to preach tolerance, Herzen *broke* with that liberal sage. Herzen turned upon Kavelin's 'meagre, absurd, harmful pamphlet' written for the private guidance of a government pretending to be liberal; he denounced Kavelin's 'sentimental political maxims' which represented 'the Russian people as cattle and the government as an embodiment of intelligence'. *Kolokol* printed an article entitled 'Epitaph', which lashed out against 'professors weaving the rotten cobweb of their superciliously paltry ideas, ex-professors, once open-hearted and subsequently embittered because they saw that the healthy youth could not sympathise with their scrofulous thinking'. Kavelin at once recognised himself in this portrait.

When Chernyshevsky was arrested, the vile liberal Kavelin wrote: 'I see nothing shocking in the arrests . . . the revolutionary party considers all means fair to overthrow the government, and the latter defends itself by its own means.' As if in retort to this Cadet, Herzen wrote concerning Chernyshevsky's trial: 'And here are wretches, weed-like people, jellyfish, who say that we must not reprove the gang of robbers and scoundrels that is governing us.'

When the liberal Turgenev wrote a private letter to Alexander II assuring him of his loyalty, and donated two gold pieces for the soldiers wounded during the suppression of the Polish insurrection, *Kolokol* wrote of 'the grey-haired Magdalen (of the masculine gender) who wrote to the tsar to tell him that she knew no sleep because she was tormented by the thought that the tsar was not aware of the repentance that had overcome her'. And Turgenev at once recognised himself.

When the whole band of Russian liberals scurried away from Herzen for his defence of Poland, when the whole of 'educated society' turned its back on *Kolokol*, Herzen was not dismayed. He went on championing the freedom of Poland and lashing the suppressors, the butchers, the hangmen in the service of Alexander II. Herzen saved the honour of Russian democracy.

'We have saved the honour of the Russian name', he wrote to Turgenev, 'and for doing so we have suffered at the hands of the slavish majority.'

When it was reported that a serf peasant had killed a land-lord for an attempt to dishonour the serf's betrothed, Herzen commented in *Kolokol*: 'Well done.' When it was reported that army officers would be appointed to supervise the 'peaceable' progress of 'emancipation', Herzen wrote: 'The first wise colonel who with his unit joins the peasants instead of crushing them, will ascend the throne of the Romanovs.' When Colonel Reitern shot himself in Warsaw (1860) because he did not want to be a helper of hangmen, Herzen wrote: 'If there is to be any shooting, the ones to be shot should be the generals who give orders to fire upon unarmed people.' When fifty peasants were massacred in Bezdna, and their leader, Anton Petrov, was executed (12 April 1861), Herzen wrote in *Kolokol*:

> If only my words could reach you, toiler and sufferer of the land of Russia! . . . How well I would teach you to despise your spiritual shepherds, placed over you by the St Peters-burg Synod and a German tsar. . . . You hate the landlord, you hate the official, you fear them, and rightly so; but you still believe in the tsar and the bishop. . . .. Do not believe them. The tsar is with them and they are his men. It is him you now see – you, the father of a youth murdered in Bezdna, and you, the son of a father murdered in Penza. . . . Your shepherds are as ignorant as you, and as poor. . . . Such was another Anthony (not Bishop Anthony, but Anton of Bezdna) who suffered for you in Kazan. . . . The miracles, and praying to them will not cure a tooth-ache but their living memory may produce one miracle – your emancipation.

This shows how infamously and vilely Herzen is being slandered by our liberals entrenched in the slavish 'legal' press, who magnify Herzen's weak points and say nothing about his strong points. It was not Herzen's fault but his misfortune that he could not see the revolutionary people in Russia itself in the 1840s. When *in the sixties* he came to see the revolutionary people, he sided fearlessly with the revolutionary democracy against liberalism. He fought for a victory of the people over tsarism, not for a deal between the liberal bourgeoisie and the landlords' tsar. He raised aloft the banner of revolution.

In commemorating Herzen, we clearly see the three generations, the three classes, that were active in the Russian revolution. At first it was nobles and landlords, the Decembrists and Herzen. These revolutionaries formed but a narrow group. They were very far removed from the people. But their effort was not in vain. The Decembrists awakened Herzen. Herzen began the work of revolutionary agitation.

This work was taken up, extended, strengthened and tempered by the revolutionary *raznochintsi* from Chernyshevsky to the heroes of *Narodnaya Volya*. The range of fighters widened, their contact with the people became closer. 'The young helmsmen of the gathering storm' is what Herzen called them. But it was not yet the storm itself.

The storm is the movement of the masses themselves. The proletariat, the only class that is thoroughly revolutionary, rose at the head of the masses and for the first time aroused millions of peasants to open revolutionary struggle. The first onslaught in this storm took place in 1905. The next is beginning to develop under our very eyes. In commemorating Herzen, the proletariat is learning from his example to appreciate the great importance of revolutionary theory. It is learning that selfless devotion to the revolution and revolutionary propaganda among the people is not wasted even if long decades divide the sowing from the harvest. It is learning to ascertain the role of the various classes in the Russian and in the international revolution. Enriched by these lessons, the proletariat will fight its way to a free alliance with the socialist workers of all lands, having crushed that loathsome monster, the tsarist monarchy, against which Herzen was the first to raise the great banner of struggle by addressing his *free Russian word* to the masses[3].

LEO TOLSTOY AS THE MIRROR OF THE RUSSIAN REVOLUTION

To identify the great artist with the revolution which he has obviously failed to understand, and from which he obviously stands aloof, may at first sight seem strange and artificial. A mirror which does not reflect things correctly could hardly be called a mirror. Our revolution, however, is an extremely complicated thing. Among the mass of those who are directly making it and participating in it, there are many social elements which also stand aloof from the real historical tasks with which the course of events has confronted them. And if we have before us a really great artist, he must have reflected, in his work, at least some of the essential aspects of the revolution.

The legal Russian press, though its pages teem with articles, letters and comments on Tolstoy's eightieth birthday, is least of all interested in analysing his works from the standpoint of the character of the Russian revolution and its motive forces. The whole of this press is steeped to nausea in hypocrisy, hypocrisy of a double kind: official and liberal. The former is the crude hypocrisy of the venal hack who was ordered yesterday to hound Leo Tolstoy and today to show that Tolstoy is a patriot, and to try to observe the decencies before the eyes of Europe. That the hacks of this kind have been paid for their screeds is common knowledge and they cannot deceive anybody. Much more refined and therefore much more pernicious and dangerous is liberal hypocrisy. To listen to the Cadet Balalaikins* of *Rech*, one would think that their sympathy for Tolstoy is of the most complete and ardent kind. Actually, their calculated declamations and pompous phrases about the 'great seeker after God' are false from beginning to end, for no Russian liberal believes in Tolstoy's god or sympathises with Tolstoy's criticism of the existing social order. He associates himself with a popular name in order to increase his political capital, in order to

* Balalaikin – a character in *A Modern Idyll* by Saltykov-Shchedryn, a liberal windbag.

pose as a leader of the nationwide opposition; he seeks, with the din of thunder and claptrap, to *drown* the demand for a straight and clear answer to the question: what are the glaring contradictions of 'Tolstoyism' due to, and what shortcomings and weaknesses of our revolution do they express?

The contradictions in Tolstoy's works, views, doctrines, in his school, are indeed glaring. On the one hand, we have the great artist, the genius who has not only drawn incomparable pictures of Russian life but has made first-class contributions to world literature. On the other hand, we have the landlord obsessed with Christ. On the one hand, the remarkably powerful, forthright and sincere protest against social falsehood and hypocrisy; and on the other, the 'Tolstoyan', that is the jaded, hysterical sniveller called the Russian intellectual, who publicly beats his breast and wails: 'I am a bad, wicked man, but I am practising moral self-perfection; I don't eat meat any more, I now eat rice cutlets.' On the one hand, merciless criticism of capitalist exploitation, exposure of government outrage, the farcical courts and State administration, and unmasking of the profound contradictions between the growth of wealth and achievements of civilisation and the growth of poverty, degradation and misery among the working masses. On the other, the crackpot preaching submission, 'resist not evil' with violence. On the one hand, the most sober realism, the tearing away of all and sundry masks; on the other, the preaching of one of the most odious things on earth, namely religion, the striving to replace officially appointed priests by priests who will serve from moral conviction, that is to cultivate the most refined and, therefore, particularly disgusting clericalism. Verily:

> Thou art poor, yet thou art rich,
> Thou art mighty yet thou art powerless –
> – Mother Russia!

That Tolstoy, owing to these contradictions, could not possibly understand either the working-class movement and its role in the struggle for socialism, or the Russian revolution, goes without saying. But the contradictions in Tolstoy's views and doctrines are not accidental; they express the contradictory conditions of Russian life in the last third of the nineteenth century. The patriarchal countryside, only recently emancipated from serfdom, was literally given over to the capitalist and the tax collector to be fleeced and plundered. The ancient foundations of peasant economy and peasant life, foundations that had really held for centuries, were broken up for scrap with extraordinary rapidity. And the contradictions in Tolstoy's views must be appraised not from the standpoint of the present-day working-class movement and present-day socialism (such an appraisal is, of course, needed, but it is not enough), but from the standpoint of protest against advancing capitalism, against the ruining of the masses, dispossessed of their land – a protest which had to arise from the patriarchal Russian countryside. Tolstoy is absurd as a prophet who has discovered new nostrums for the salvation of mankind – and therefore the foreign and Russian 'Tolstoyans' who have sought to convert the weakest side of his doctrine into a dogma, are not worth speaking of. Tolstoy is great as the spokesman of the ideas and sentiments that emerged among the millions of Russian peasants at the time of the bourgeois revolution's approach in Russia. Tolstoy is original, because the sum total of his views, taken as a whole, happens to express the specific features of our revolution as a *peasant* bourgeois revolution. From this point of view, the contradictions in Tolstoy's views are indeed a mirror of those contradictory conditions in which the peasantry had to play their historical part in our revolution. On the one hand, centuries of feudal oppression and decades of accelerated post-Reform pauperisation piled up mountains of hate, resentment, and desperate determination. The striving to sweep away completely the official Church, the landlords and the landlord government, to destroy all the old forms and ways of land ownership, to clear the land, to replace the police-class State by a community of free and equal small peasants – this striving is the keynote of every historical step the peasantry has taken in our revolution; and, undoubtedly, the message of Tolstoy's writings conforms to this peasant striving far more than it does to abstract 'Christian anarchism', as his 'system' of views is sometimes appraised.

On the other hand, the peasantry, striving towards new ways of life, had a very crude, patriarchal, semi-religious idea of what kind of life this should be, by what struggle could liberty be won, what leaders it could have in this struggle, what was the attitude of the bourgeoisie and the bourgeois intelligentsia towards the interests of peasant-revolution, why the forcible overthrow of tsarist rule was needed to abolish landlordism. The whole past life of the peasantry had taught it to hate the landowner and the official but it did not, and could not, teach it where to seek an answer to all these questions. In our revolution a minor part of the peasantry really did fight, did organise to some extent for this purpose: and a very small part indeed rose up in arms to exterminate its enemies, to destroy the tsar's servants and protectors of the landlords. Most of the peasantry wept and prayed, moralised and dreamed, wrote petitions and sent 'pleaders' – quite in the vein of Leo Tolstoy! And, as always happens in such cases, the effect of this Tolstoyan abstention from politics, this Tolstoyan renunciation of politics, this lack of interest in and understanding of politics, was that only a minority followed the lead of the class-conscious revolutionary proletariat, while the majority became the prey of those unprincipled, servile, bourgeois intellectuals who under the name of Cadets hastened from a meeting of Trudoviks to Stolypin's anteroom, and begged, haggled, agreed, made peace and promised to keep it – until they were kicked out with a military jackboot. Tolstoy's ideas are a mirror of the weakness, the shortcomings of our peasant revolt, a reflection of the flabbiness of the patriarchal countryside and of the hidebound cowardice of the 'enterprising moujik'.[4]

L. N. TOLSTOY AND THE MODERN LABOUR MOVEMENT

November 1910

The Russian workers in practically all the large cities of Russia have already reacted to the death of L. N. Tolstoy and, in one way or another, expressed their attitude to the writer who produced a number of most remarkable works of art that put him in the ranks of the great writers of the world, and to the thinker who with immense power, self-confidence and sincerity *raised* a number of questions concerning the basic features of the modern political and social system. All in all, this attitude was expressed in the telegram, printed in the newspapers, which was sent by the labour deputies in the Third Duma.

L. Tolstoy began his literary career when serfdom still existed but at a time when it had already obviously come to the end of its days. Tolstoy's main activity falls in that period of Russian history which lies between two of its turning points, 1861 and 1905.* Throughout this period traces of serfdom, direct survivals of it, permeated the whole economic (particularly in the countryside) and political life of the country. And at the same time this was a period of the accelerated growth of capitalism from below and its implantation from above.

In what were the survivals of serfdom expressed? Most of all and clearest of all is the fact that in Russia, mainly an agricultural country, agriculture at that time was in the hands of a ruined, impoverished peasantry who were using antiquated, primitive methods on the old feudal allotments which had been cut off in 1861 for the benefit of the landlords. And, on the other hand, agriculture was in the hands of the landlords who in Central Russia cultivated the land by the labour, the wooden ploughs, and the horses of the peasants in return for the 'cut-off

---

* In February 1861 Tsar Alexander II freed the Russian peasants from serfdom, but on their emancipation they had to yield to the gentry much of the land they had worked; for the small amount of land they retained, they had to pay a heavy price. As 'free men' they were crushed by debts, poverty and homelessness.

lands', meadows, access to watering places, etc. To all intents and purposes this was the old feudal system of economy. Throughout this period the political system of Russia was also permeated with feudalism. This is evident from the constitution of the state prior to the first moves to change it in 1905, from the predominant influence of the landed nobility on state affairs, and from the unlimited power of the officials, who also for the most part – especially the higher ranks – came from the landed nobility.

After 1861 this old patriarchal Russia began rapidly to disintegrate under the influence of world capitalism. The peasants were starving, dying off, being ruined as never before, fleeing to the towns and abandoning the soil. There was a boom in the construction of railways, mills, factories, thanks to the 'cheap labour' of the ruined peasants. Big finance capital was developing in Russia together with large-scale commerce and industry.

It was this rapid, painful, drastic demolition of all the old 'pillars' of old Russia that was reflected in the works of Tolstoy the artist, and in the views of Tolstoy the thinker.

Tolstoy had an unsurpassed knowledge of rural Russia, the mode of life of the landlords and peasants. In his artistic productions he gave descriptions of this life that are numbered among the best in world literature. The drastic demolition of all the 'old pillars' of rural Russia sharpened his attention, deepened his interest in what was going on around him, and led to a radical change in his whole world outlook. By birth and education Tolstoy belonged to the highest landed nobility in Russia – he broke with all the customary views of his environment and in his later works attacked with fierce criticism all the contemporary state, church, social and economic institutions which were based on the enslavement of the masses, on their poverty, on the ruin of the peasants and the petty proprietors in general, on the coercion and hypocrisy which permeated all contemporary life from top to bottom.

Tolstoy's criticism was not new. He said nothing that had not been said long before him both in European and in Russian literature by friends of the working people. But the uniqueness of Tolstoy's criticism and its historical significance lie in the fact that it expressed, with a power such as is possessed only by artists of genius, the radical change in the views of the broadest masses of the people in Russia of this period, namely, rural, peasant Russia. For Tolstoy's criticism of contemporary institutions differs from the criticism of the same institutions by representatives of the modern labour movement in the fact that Tolstoy's point of view was that of the patriarchal, naïve peasant, whose psychology Tolstoy introduced into his criticism and doctrine. Tolstoy's criticism is marked by such emotional power, such passion, freshness, sincerity and fearlessness in striving to 'go to the roots', to find the real cause of the affliction of the masses, precisely because this criticism really expresses a sharp change in the ideas of millions of peasants, who had only just emerged from feudalism into freedom, and saw that this freedom meant new horrors of ruin, death by starvation, a homeless life among the lower strata of the city population, and so on and so forth. Tolstoy mirrored their sentiments so faithfully that he imported their naïvety into his own doctrine, their alienation from political life, their mysticism, their desire to keep aloof from the world, 'non-resistance to evil', their impotent imprecations against capitalism and the 'power of money'. The protest of millions of peasants and their desperation – these were combined in Tolstoy's doctrine.

The representatives of the modern labour movement find that they have plenty to protest against but nothing to despair about. Despair is typical of the classes which are perishing, but the class of wage-workers is growing inevitably, developing and becoming strong in every capitalist society, Russia included. Despair is typical of those who do not understand the causes of evil, see no way out, and are incapable of struggle. The modern industrial proletariat does not belong to the category of such classes.[5]

TOLSTOY AND THE PROLETARIAN STRUGGLE

December 1910

Tolstoy's indictment of the ruling classes was made with tremendous power and sincerity; with absolute clarity he laid bare the inner falsehood of all those institutions by which modern society is maintained: the Church, the law courts, militarism, 'lawful' wedlock, bourgeois science. But his doctrine proved to be in complete contradiction to the life, work and struggle of the grave-digger of the modern social system, the proletariat. Whose then was the point of view reflected in the teachings of Leo Tolstoy? Through his lips there spoke that multitudinous mass of the Russian people who *already* detest the masters of modern life but have not *yet* advanced to the point of intelligent, consistent, thoroughgoing, implacable struggle against them.

The history and the outcome of the great Russian revolution have shown that such precisely was the mass that found itself *between* the class-conscious, socialist proletariat and the out-and-out defenders of the old regime. This mass, consisting mainly of the peasantry, showed in the revolution how great was its hatred of the old, how keenly it felt all the inflictions of the modern regime, how great within it was the spontaneous yearning . . . to find a better life.

At the same time, however, this mass showed in the revolution that it was not politically conscious enough in its hatred, that it was not consistent in its struggle and that its quest for a better life was confined within narrow bounds. This great human ocean, agitated to its very depths, with all its weaknesses and all its strong features, found its reflection in the doctrine of Tolstoy.

By studying the literary works of Leo Tolstoy, the Russian working class will learn to know its enemies better, but in examining the *doctrine* of Tolstoy, the whole Russian people will have to understand where their own weakness lies, the weakness which did not allow them to carry the cause of their emancipation to its conclusion. This must be understood in order to go forward.

This advance is impeded by all those who declare Tolstoy a 'universal conscience', a 'teacher of life'. This is a lie that the liberals are deliberately spreading in their desire to utilise the anti-revolutionary aspect of Tolstoy's doctrine. This lie about Tolstoy as a 'teacher of life' is being repeated after the liberals by some former Social-Democrats.

The Russian people will secure their emancipation only when they realise that it is not from Tolstoy that they must learn to win a better life but from the class which Tolstoy did not understand, and which alone is capable of destroying the old world which Tolstoy hated. That class is the proletariat.[6]

LEO TOLSTOY AND HIS EPOCH

January 1911

The epoch to which Leo Tolstoy belongs and which is reflected in such bold relief in his brilliant literary works and in his teachings began after 1861 and lasted until 1905. True, Tolstoy commenced his literary career earlier and it ended later, but it was during this period, whose transitional nature gave rise to all the distinguishing features of Tolstoy's works and of Tolstoyism, that he fully matured both as an artist and as a thinker.

Through Levin, a character in *Anna Karenina*, Tolstoy very vividly expressed the nature of the turn in Russia's history that took place during this half-century.

'The talk about the harvest, hiring labourers, and so forth, which, as Levin knew, it was the custom to regard as something very low . . . now seemed to Levin to be the only important thing. "This, perhaps was unimportant under serfdom, or is unimportant in England. In both cases the conditions are definite; but here today, when everything has been turned upside down and is only just taking shape again, the question of how these conditions will shape is the only important question in Russia", mused Levin.' 'Here in Russia everything has now been turned upside down and is only just taking shape' – it is difficult to imagine a more apt characterisation of the period 1861–1905. What 'was turned upside down' is familiar, or at least well known, to every Russian. It was serfdom, and the whole of the 'old order' that went with it. What 'is just taking shape' is totally unknown, alien and incomprehensible to the broad masses of the population. Tolstoy conceived this bourgeois order which was 'only just taking shape' vaguely, in the form of a bogey-England. Truly, a bogey, because Tolstoy rejects, on principle so to speak, any attempt to investigate the features of the social system in this 'England', the connection between this system and the domination of capital, the role played by money, the rise and development of exchange. Like the Narodniks, he refuses to see, he shuts his eyes to, and dismisses the thought that what is 'taking shape' in Russia is none other than the bourgeois system.

It is true that, if not the 'only important' question, then certainly one of the most important from the standpoint of the immediate tasks of all social and political activities in Russia in the period 1861–1905 (and in our times, too) was that of 'what shape' this system would take, this bourgeois system that had assumed extremely varied forms in 'England', Germany, America, France and so forth. But such a definite, concretely historical presentation of the question was something absolutely foreign to Tolstoy. He reasons in the abstract, he recognises only the standpoint of the 'eternal' principles of morality, the eternal truths of religion, failing to realise that this standpoint is merely the ideological reflection of the old ('turned upside down') order, the feudal order, the way of life of the Oriental peoples.

In *Lucerne* (written in 1857), Tolstoy declares that to regard 'civilisation' as a boon is an 'imaginary concept' which 'destroys in human nature the instinctive, most blissful primitive need for good'. 'We have only one infallible guide', exclaims Tolstoy, 'the Universal Spirit that permeates us.'

In *The Slavery of Our Times* (written in 1900), Tolstoy, repeating still more zealously these appeals to the Universal Spirit, declares that political economy is a 'pseudo science' because it takes as the 'pattern' 'little England, where conditions are most exceptional', instead of taking as a pattern 'the conditions of men in the whole world throughout the whole of history'. What this 'whole world' is like is revealed to us in the article 'Progress and the Definition of Education' (1862). Tolstoy counters the opinion of the historians that progress is 'a general law for mankind' by referring to 'the whole of what is known as the Orient'. There is no general law of human progress, says Tolstoy, and this is proved by the quiescence of the Oriental peoples.

Tolstoyism, in its real historical content, is an ideology of an Oriental, an Asiatic order. Hence the asceticism, the non-resistance to evil, the profound notes of pessimism, the conviction that 'everything is nothing, everything is a material nothing' ('The Meaning of Life'), and faith in the 'Spirit', in the beginning of everything, and that man, in his relations to this beginning, is merely a 'labourer ... allotted the task of saving his own soul', etc. Tolstoy is true to this ideology in his *Kreutzer Sonata* too when he says: 'the emancipation of woman lies not in colleges and not in parliaments, but in the bedroom', and in the article written in 1862, in which he says that universities train only 'irritable, debilitated liberals' for whom 'the people have no use at all', who are 'uselessly torn from their former environment,' find no place in life, and so forth.

Pessimism, non-resistance, appeal to the 'Spirit', constitute an ideology inevitable in an epoch when the whole of the old order 'has been turned upside down', and when the masses, who have been brought up under this old order, who imbibed with their mother's milk the principles, the habits, the traditions and beliefs of this order, do not and cannot see what kind of a new order is 'taking shape', what social forces are capable of bringing release from the incalculable and exceptionally acute distress that is characteristic of epochs of 'upheaval'.

The period of 1862–1904 was just such a period of upheaval in Russia, a period in which, before everyone's eyes, the old order collapsed, never to be restored, in which the new system was only just taking shape. The social forces shaping the new system first manifested themselves on a broad, nationwide scale, in mass public action in the most varied fields only in 1905. And the events in 1905 in Russia were followed by analogous events in a number of countries in that very 'Orient' to the 'quiescence' of which Tolstoy referred in 1862. The year 1905 marked the beginning of the end of 'Oriental' quiescence. Precisely for this reason that year marked the historical end of Tolstoyism, the end of an epoch that could give rise to Tolstoy's teachings and in which they were inevitable, not as something individual, not as a caprice or a fad, but as the ideology of the conditions of life under which millions and millions actually found themselves for a certain period of time.

Tolstoy's doctrine is certainly utopian and in content is reactionary in the most precise and most profound sense of the word. But that certainly does not mean that the doctrine was not socialistic or that it did not contain critical elements capable of providing valuable material for the enlightenment of the advanced classes.

There are various kinds of socialism. In all countries where the capitalist mode of production prevails there is a socialism which expresses the ideology of the class that is going to take the place of the bourgeoisie; and there is the socialism that expresses the ideology of the classes that are going to be replaced by the bourgeoisie. Feudal socialism, for example is socialism of the latter type, and the nature of this socialism was appraised long ago, over sixty years ago, by Marx, simultaneously with his appraisal of other types of socialism.

Furthermore, critical elements are inherent in Tolstoy's utopian doctrine, just as they are inherent in many utopian systems. But we must not forget Marx's profound observation to the effect that the value of critical elements in utopian socialism 'bears an inverse relation to historical development'. The more the activities of the social forces which are shaping the new Russia and bringing release from present-day social evils develop and assume a definite character, the more rapidly is critical-utopian socialism losing all practical value and all theoretical justification.

A quarter of a century ago, the critical elements in Tolstoy's doctrine might at times have been of practical value for some sections of the population in spite of their reactionary and utopian features. This could not have been the case during, say, the last decade, because historical development had made considerable progress between the eighties and the end of the last century. In our days, since the series of events mentioned above has put an end to 'Oriental' quiescence, in our days, when the consciously reactionary ideas of *Vekhi* (reactionary in the narrow-class, selfishly-class sense) have become so enormously widespread among the liberal bourgeoisie and when these ideas have infected even a section of those who were almost Marxists and have created a liquidationist trend – in our days, the most direct and most profound harm is caused by every attempt to idealise Tolstoy's doctrine, to justify or to mitigate his 'non-resistance', his appeals to the 'Spirit', his exhortations for 'moral self-perfection', his doctrine of 'conscience' and universal 'love', his preachings of asceticism and quietism, and so forth.[7]

V. I. LENIN

LESSONS OF THE PARIS COMMUNE

18 March 1908

After the *coup d'état* which marked the end of the revolution of 1848, France fell under the yoke of the Napoleonic regime for a period of eighteen years. This regime brought upon the country not only economic ruin but national humiliation. In rising against the old regime the proletariat undertook two tasks – one of them national and the other of class character – the liberation of France from the German invasion and the socialist emancipation of the workers from capitalism. This union of two tasks forms a unique feature of the Commune.

The bourgeoisie had formed a 'government of national defence' and the proletariat had to fight for national independence under its leadership. Actually, it was a government of 'national betrayal' which saw its mission in fighting the Paris proletariat. But the proletariat, blinded by patriotic illusions, did not perceive this. The patriotic idea had its origin in the Great Revolution of the eighteenth century; it swayed the minds of the socialists of the Commune; and Blanqui, for example, undoubtedly a revolutionary and an ardent supporter of socialism, could find no better title for his newspaper than the bourgeois cry: '*The country is in danger!*'

Combining contradictory tasks – patriotism and socialism – was the fatal mistake of the French socialists. In the Manifesto of the International, issued in September 1870, Marx had warned the French proletariat against being misled by a false national idea; profound changes had taken place since the Great Revolution, class antagonisms had sharpened, and whereas at that time the struggle against the whole of European reaction united the entire revolutionary nation, now the proletariat could no longer combine its interests with the interests of other classes hostile to it; let the bourgeoisie bear the responsibility for the national humiliation – the task of the proletariat was to fight for the socialist emancipation of labour from the yoke of the bourgeoisie.

And indeed, the true nature of the bourgeois 'patriotism' was not long in revealing itself. Having concluded an ignominious peace with the Prussians, the Versailles government proceeded to its immediate task – it launched an attack to wrest the arms that terrified it from the hands of the Paris proletariat. The workers replied by proclaiming the Commune and civil war.

Although the socialist proletariat was split up into numerous sects, the Commune was a splendid example of the unanimity with which the proletariat was able to accomplish the democratic tasks which the bourgeoisie could only proclaim. Without any particularly complex legislation, in a simple straightforward manner, the proletariat, which had seized power, carried out the democratisation of the social system, abolished the bureaucracy, and made all official posts elective.

But two mistakes destroyed the fruits of the splendid victory. The proletariat stopped half-way: instead of setting about 'expropriating the expropriators', it allowed itself to be led astray by dreams of establishing a higher justice in the country united by a common national task; such institutions as the banks, for example, were not taken over, the Proudhonist theories about a 'just exchange' etc. still prevailed among the socialists. The second mistake was excessive magnanimity on the part of the proletariat: instead of destroying its enemies, it sought to exert moral influence on them; it underestimated the significance of direct military operations in civil war, and instead of launching a resolute offensive against Versailles that would have crowned its victory in Paris, it tarried and gave the Versailles government time to gather the dark forces and prepare for the bloodsoaked week of May.

But despite all its mistakes the Commune was a superb example of the great proletarian movement of the nineteenth century. Marx set a high value on the historic significance of the Commune – if, during the treacherous attempt by the Versailles gang to seize the arms of the Paris proletariat, the workers had allowed themselves to be disarmed without a fight, the disastrous effect of the demoralisation that this weakness would have caused in the proletarian movement would have been far, far greater than the losses suffered by the working class in the battle to defend its arms. The sacrifices of the Commune, heavy as they were, are made up for by its significance for the general struggle of the proletariat: it stirred the socialist movement throughout Europe, it demonstrated the strength of civil war, it dispelled patriotic illusions, and destroyed the naïve belief in any efforts of the bourgeoisie for common national aims. The Commune taught the European proletariat to consider concretely the tasks of the socialist revolution.

The lesson learnt by the proletariat will not be forgotten. The working class will make use of it, as it has already done in Russia during the December uprising.

The period that preceded the Russian revolution and prepared for it bears a certain resemblance to the period of the Napoleonic yoke in France. In Russia, too, the autocratic clique has brought upon the country economic ruin and national humiliation. But the outbreak of revolution was held back for a long time since social development had not yet created conditions for a mass movement and, notwithstanding all the courage displayed, the isolated actions against the government in the pre-revolutionary period were defeated by the apathy of the masses. Only the Social-Democrats, by strenuous and systematic work, educated the masses to the level of the higher forms of struggle – mass action and civil war.

The Social-Democrats were able to shatter the 'common national' and 'patriotic' delusions of the young proletariat, and later, when the Manifesto of 17 October [1905] had been wrested from the tsar due to their direct intervention, the proletariat began vigorous preparations for the next, inevitable phase of the revolution – the armed uprising. Having shed 'common national' illusions, it concentrated its class forces in its own mass organisations – the Soviets of Workers' and Soldiers' Deputies, etc. And notwithstanding all the differences in the aims and tasks of the Russian revolution compared with the French revolution of 1871, the Russian proletariat had to resort to the same method of struggle as that first used by the Paris Commune – civil war. Mindful of the lessons of the Commune, it knew that the proletariat should not ignore peaceful methods of struggle – they serve its ordinary, day-to-day interests, they are necessary in periods of preparation for revolution – but it must never forget that in certain conditions the class struggle assumes the form of armed conflict and civil war; there are times when the interests of the proletariat call for ruthless extermination of its enemies in open armed clashes. This was first demonstrated by the French proletariat in the Commune and brilliantly confirmed by the Russian proletariat in the December uprising.

And although these magnificent uprisings of the working class were crushed, there will be another uprising, in the face of which the forces of the enemies of the proletariat will prove ineffective, and from which the socialist proletariat will emerge completely victorious.[8]

IN MEMORY OF THE PARIS COMMUNE

1911

Forty years have passed since the proclamation of the Paris Commune. In accordance with tradition, the French workers paid homage to the memory of the men and women of the revolution of 18 March 1871, by meetings and demonstrations. At the end of May they will again place wreaths on the graves of the Communards who were shot, the victims of the terrible 'May Week', and over their graves they will once more vow to fight untiringly until their ideas have triumphed and the cause they bequeathed has been fully achieved.

Why does the proletariat, not only in France but throughout the entire world, honour the men and women of the Paris Commune as their predecessors? And what is the heritage of the Commune? The Commune sprang up spontaneously. No one consciously prepared it in an organised way. The unsuccessful war with Germany, the privations suffered during the siege, the unemployment among the proletariat and the ruin among the lower middle classes, the indignation of the masses against the upper classes and against authorities who had displayed utter incompetence, the unrest among the working class, which was discontented with its lot and was striving for a different social system, the reactionary composition of the National Assembly, which roused apprehensions as to the fate of the republic – all this and many other factors combined to drive the population of Paris to revolution on 18 March, which unexpectedly placed power in the hands of the National Guard, in the hands of the working class and the petty bourgeoisie which had sided with it.

It was an event unprecedented in history. Up to that time power had, as a rule, been in the hands of landowners and capitalists, that is, in the hands of their trusted agents who made up the so-called government. After the revolution of 18 March, when M. Thiers's government had fled from Paris with its troops, its police and its officials, the people became masters of the situation and power passed into the hands of the proletariat. But in modern society, the proletariat, economically enslaved by capital, cannot dominate politically unless it breaks the chains which fetter it to capital. That is why the movement of the Commune was bound to take on a socialist tinge, that is, to strive to overthrow the rule of the bourgeoisie, the rule of capital, and to destroy the very foundations of the contemporary social order.

At first this movement was extremely indefinite and confused. It was joined by patriots who hoped that the Commune would renew the war with the Germans and bring it to a successful conclusion. It enjoyed the support of the small shopkeepers who were threatened with ruin unless there was a postponement of payments of debts and rent (the government refused to grant this postponement, but they obtained it from the Commune). Finally, it enjoyed, at first, the sympathy of bourgeois republicans who feared that the reactionary National Assembly (the 'rustics', the savage landlords) would restore the monarchy. But it was of course the workers (especially the artisans of Paris), among whom active socialist propaganda had been carried on during the last years of the Second Empire and many of whom even belonged to the International, who played the principal part in this movement.

Only the workers remained loyal to the Commune to the end. The bourgeois republicans and the petty bourgeoisie soon broke away from it: the former were frightened off by the revolutionary-socialist, proletarian character of the movement; the latter broke away when they saw that it was doomed to inevitable defeat. Only the French proletarians supported *their* government fearlessly and untiringly, they alone fought and died for it – that is to say, for the cause of the emancipation of the working class, for a better future for all toilers.

Deserted by its former allies and left without support, the Commune was doomed to defeat. The entire bourgeoisie of France, all the landlords, stockbrokers, factory owners, all the robbers, great and small, all the exploiters joined forces against it. This bourgeois coalition, supported by Bismarck (who released 100,000 French prisoners of war to help crush revolutionary Paris), succeeded in rousing the ignorant peasants and the petty bourgeoisie of the provinces against the proletariat of Paris, and forming a ring of steel around half of Paris (the other half was besieged by the German army). In some of the larger cities in France (Marseilles, Lyons, St Etienne, Dijon, etc.) the workers also attempted to seize power, to proclaim the Commune and come to the help of Paris; but these attempts were short-lived. Paris, which had first raised the banner of proletarian revolt, was left to its own resources and doomed to certain destruction.

Two conditions, at least, are necessary for a victorious social revolution – highly developed productive forces and a proletariat adequately prepared for it. But in 1871 both of these conditions were lacking. French capitalism was still poorly developed, and France was at that time mainly a petty-bourgeois country (artisans, peasants, shopkeepers, etc.). On the other hand, there was no workers' party; the working class had not gone through a long school of struggle and was unprepared, and for the most part did not even clearly visualise its tasks and the methods of fulfilling them. There was no serious political organisation of the proletariat, nor were there strong trade unions and co-operative societies. . . .

But the chief thing which the Commune lacked was time – an opportunity to take stock of the situation and to embark upon the fulfilment of its programme. It had scarcely had time to start work, when the government, entrenched in Versailles and supported by the entire bourgeoisie, began hostilities against Paris. The Commune had to concentrate primarily on self-defence. Right up to the very end, 21–28 May, it had no time to think seriously of anything else.

However, in spite of these unfavourable conditions, in spite of its brief existence, the Commune managed to promulgate a few measures which sufficiently characterise its real significance and aims. The Commune did away with the standing army, that blind weapon in the hands of the ruling classes and armed the whole people. It proclaimed the separation of Church and State, abolished State payments to religious bodies (that is, State salaries for priests), made popular education purely secular, and in this way struck a severe blow at the gendarmes in cassocks. In the purely social sphere the Commune accomplished very little, but this little nevertheless clearly reveals its character as a popular, workers' government. Night-work in bakeries was forbidden; the system of fines, which represented legalised robbery of the workers, was abolished. Finally there was the famous decree that all factories and workshops abandoned or shut down by their owners were to be turned over to associations of workers that were to resume production. And, as if to emphasise its character as a truly democratic, proletarian government, the Commune decreed that the salaries of all administrative and government officials, irrespective of rank, should not exceed the normal wages of a worker, and in no case amount to more than 6,000 francs a year.

All these measures showed clearly enough that the Commune was a deadly menace to the old world founded on the enslavement and exploitation of the people. That was why bourgeois society could not feel at ease so long as the Red Flag of the proletariat flew above the *Hôtel de Ville* in Paris. And when the organised forces of the government finally succeeded in gaining the upper hand over the poorly organised forces of the revolution, the Bonapartist generals, who had been beaten by the Germans and who showed courage only in fighting their defeated countrymen, those French Rennenkampfs and Meller-Zakomelskys, organised such a slaughter as Paris had never known. About 30,000 Parisians were shot down by the bestial soldiery, and about 45,000 were arrested, many of whom were afterwards executed, while thousands were transported or exiled. In all, Paris lost about 100,000 of its best people, including some of the finest workers in all trades.

The bourgeoisie were satisfied. 'Now we have finished with socialism for a long time', said their leader, the bloodthirsty dwarf, Thiers, after he and his generals had drowned the proletariat of Paris in blood. But these bourgeois crows croaked in vain. Less than six years after the suppression of the Commune, when many of its champions were still pining in prison or in exile, a new working-class movement arose in France. A new socialist generation, enriched by the experience of their predecessors and not a bit discouraged by their defeat, picked up the flag which had fallen from the hands of the fighters in the cause of the Commune and bore it boldly and confidently forward. Their battle-cry was: 'Long live the social revolution', 'Long live the Commune'. And in another few years, the new workers' party and the agitational work launched by it through-out the country compelled the ruling classes to release the Communards who were still kept in prison by the government.

The memory of the fighters of the Commune is honoured not only by the workers of France but also by the proletariat of the whole world. For the Commune fought, not for some local or narrow national aim, but for the emancipation of all toiling humanity, of all those downtrodden and oppressed. As a fore-most fighter for the social revolution, the Commune has won sympathy wherever there is a proletariat suffering and engaged in a struggle. The epic of its life and death, the sight of a work-ers' government which seized the capital of the world and held it for over two months, the spectacle of the heroic struggle of the proletariat and the torments it underwent after its defeat – all this raised the spirit of millions of workers, aroused their hopes and enlisted their sympathy for the cause of socialism. The thunder of the cannon in Paris awakened the most backward sections of the proletariat from their deep slumber, and every-where gave impetus to the growth of revolutionary socialist propaganda. That is why the cause of the Commune is not dead. It lives to the present day in every one of us.

The cause of the Commune is the cause of the social revolu-tion, the cause of the complete political and economic emanci-pation of the toilers. It is the cause of the proletariat of the whole world. And in this sense it is immortal.[9]

PARTY ORGANISATION AND PARTY LITERATURE

November 1905

The new conditions for Social-Democratic work in Russia which have arisen since the October revolution [1905] have brought the question of party literature to the fore. The distinction between the illegal and the legal press, that miserable heritage of the epoch of feudal, autocratic Russia, is beginning to disappear. It is not yet dead, far from it. . . .

So long as there was a distinction between the illegal and the legal press, the question of the party and the non-party press was decided extremely simply and in an extremely false and abnormal way. The entire illegal press was a party press, being published by organisations and run by groups of practical party workers. The entire legal press was non-party – since parties were banned – but it 'gravitated' towards one party or another. Unnatural alliances, strange 'bed-fellows' and false cover-devices were inevitable. The forced reserve of people who wished to express party views merged with the immature thinking or mental cowardice of those who had not risen to these views and who were not, in effect, party people.

An accursed period of Aesopian language, literary bondage, slavish speech, and ideological serfdom! The proletariat has put an end to this foul atmosphere which stifled everything living and fresh in Russia. But so far, the proletariat has won only half freedom for Russia.

The revolution is not yet completed. While tsarism is *no longer* strong enough to defeat the revolution, the revolution is *not yet* strong enough to defeat tsarism. . . .

. . . the half-way revolution compels all of us to set to work at once organising the whole thing on new lines. Today literature, even that published 'legally', can be nine-tenths party literature. It must become party literature. In contradistinction to bourgeois customs, to the profit-making, commercialised bourgeois press, to bourgeois literary careerism and individualism, 'aristocratic anarchism' and drive for profit, the socialist proletariat must put forward the principle of *party literature*, must develop this principle and put it into practice as fully and as completely as possible.

What is this principle of party literature ? It is not simply that, for the socialist proletariat, literature cannot be a means of enriching individuals or groups; it cannot, in fact, be an individual undertaking independent of the common cause of the proletariat. Down with non-partisan writers! Down with literary supermen! Literature must become *part* of the common cause of the proletariat, 'a cog and a screw' of one single great Social-Democratic mechanism set in motion by the entire politically-conscious vanguard of the entire working class. Literature must become a component of organised, planned and integrated Social-Democratic party work.

'All comparisons are lame', says a German proverb. So is my comparison of literature with a cog, of a living movement with a mechanism. And I daresay there will be even hysterical intellectuals to raise a howl about such a comparison, which degrades, deadens, 'bureaucratises' the free battle of ideas, freedom of criticism, freedom of literary creation, etc., etc. Such outcries, in point of fact, would be nothing more than an expression of bourgeois-intellectual individualism. There is no doubt that literature is least of all subject to mechanical adjustment or levelling, to the rule of the majority over the minority. There is no doubt either, that in this field greater scope must be allowed for personal initiative. It is absolutely necessary to guarantee in this field greater scope for individual inclination, thought and fantasy, form and content. All this is undeniable, but it also goes to show that the literary side of the proletarian party cause cannot be mechanically identified with its other sides. This, however, does not in the least refute the proposition, alien and strange to the bourgeoisie and bourgeois-democracy, that literature must by all means and necessarily become an element of Social-Democratic party work, inseparably bound up with the other elements. Newspapers must become the organs of the various party organisations. Publishing and distributing centres, bookshops and reading-rooms, libraries and similar establishments – must all be under party control. The organised socialist proletariat must keep an eye on all this work, supervise it in its entirety, and, from beginning to end, without any exception, infuse into it the life-stream of the living proletarian cause, thereby cutting the ground from under the old, semi-Oblomov, semi-shopkeeper Russian principle: the writer does the writing, the reader does the reading.

We are not suggesting, of course, that this transformation of literary work, which has been defiled by Asiatic censorship and the European bourgeoisie, can be accomplished all at once. Far be it from us to advocate any kind of standardised system, or a solution by means of a few decrees. Cut-and-dried schemes are least of all applicable here. What is needed is that the whole of our party, and the entire politically-conscious Social-Democratic proletariat throughout Russia should become aware of this new problem, specify it clearly, and everywhere set about solving it. Emerging from the captivity of feudal censorship we have no desire to become, and shall not become, prisoners of bourgeois-shopkeeper literary relations. We want to establish, and we shall establish, a free press, free not simply from the police, but also from capital, from careerism, and what is more, free from bourgeois-anarchist individualism.

These last words may sound paradoxical, or an affront to the reader. 'What!' some intellectual, an ardent champion of liberty, may shout, 'What! You want to impose collective control on such a delicate, individual matter as literary work! You want workmen to decide questions of science, philosophy or aesthetics by a majority of votes! You deny the absolute freedom of absolutely individual ideological work!'

Calm yourselves, gentlemen! First of all, we are discussing party literature and its subordination to party control. Everyone is free to write and say whatever he likes, without any restrictions. But every voluntary association (including the party) is also free to expel members who use the name of the party to advocate anti-party views. Freedom of speech and the press must be complete. But then freedom of association must be complete too. I am bound to accord you, in the name of free speech, the full right to shout, lie and write to your heart's content. But you are bound to grant me, in the name of freedom of association, the right to enter into, or withdraw from, association with people advocating this or that view. The party is a voluntary association, which would inevitably break up, first ideologically and then physically, if it did not cleanse itself of people advocating anti-party views. And to define the border-line between party and anti-party there is the party pro-gramme, the party's resolution on tactics and its rules and, lastly, the entire experience of international Social-Democracy, the voluntary international associations of the proletariat, which has constantly brought into its parties individual elements and trends not fully consistent, not completely Marxist and not altogether correct and which, on the other hand, has constantly conducted periodical 'cleansing' of its ranks. So it will be with us too, supporters of bourgeois 'freedom of criticism' *within* the party. We are now becoming a mass party all at once, changing abruptly to an open organisation, and it is inevitable that we shall be joined by many who are inconsistent (from the Marxist standpoint). Perhaps we shall be joined even by some Christian elements, maybe even some mystics. Freedom of thought and freedom of criticism within the party will never make us forget about the freedom of organising people into those voluntary associations known as parties.

Secondly, we must say to you bourgeois individualists that your talk about absolute freedom is sheer hypocrisy. There can be no real and effective 'freedom' in a society based on the power of money, in a society in which the masses of working people live in poverty and the handful of rich live like parasites. Are you free in relation to your bourgeois publisher, Mr Writer, in relation to your bourgeois public, which demands that you provide it with pornography in novels and paintings, and prostitution as a 'supplement' to 'sacred' scenic art? This absolute freedom is a bourgeois or an anarchist phrase (since, as a world outlook, anarchism is bourgeois philosophy turned inside out). One cannot live in society and be free from society. The freedom of the bourgeois writer, artist or actress is simply masked (or hypocritically masked) dependence on the money-bag, on corruption, on prostitution.

And we socialists expose this hypocrisy and rip off the false labels, not in order to arrive at a non-class literature and art (that will be possible only in a socialist non-class society), but to contrast this hypocritically free literature, which is in reality linked to the bourgeoisie, with a really free one that will be *openly* linked to the proletariat.

It will be a free literature, because the idea of socialism and sympathy with the working people, and not greed or careerism, will bring ever new forces to its ranks. It will be a free literature, because it will serve not some satiated heroine, not the bored 'upper ten thousand' suffering from fatty degeneration, but the millions and tens of millions of working people – the flower of the country, its strength and its future. It will be a free literature, enriching the last word in the revolutionary thought of mankind with the experience and living work of the socialist proletariat, bringing about permanent interaction between the experience of the past (scientific socialism, the completion of the development of socialism from its primitive, utopian forms) and the experience of the present (the present struggle of the worker comrades).

To work then, comrades! We are faced with a new and difficult task. But it is a noble and grateful one – to organise a broad multiform and varied literature inseparably linked with the Social-Democratic working-class movement. All Social-Democratic literature must become party literature. Every newspaper, journal, publishing house, etc., must immediately set about re-organising its work, leading up to a situation in which it will, in one form or another, be integrated into one party organisation or another. Only then will 'Social-Democratic' literature really become worthy of that name, only then will it be able to fulfil its duty and, even within the framework of bourgeois society, break out of bourgeois slavery and merge with the movement of the really advanced and thoroughly revolutionary class.[10]

V. I. LENIN

WHAT CAN BE DONE FOR PUBLIC EDUCATION

July 1913

There are quite a number of rotten prejudices current in the Western countries of which Holy Mother Russia is free. They assume there, for instance, that huge public libraries, containing hundreds of thousands and millions of volumes, should certainly not be reserved only for the handful of scholars or would-be scholars that uses them. Over there they have set themselves the strange, incomprehensible and barbaric aim of making these gigantic, boundless libraries available, not to a guild of scholars, professors and other such specialists, but to the masses, to the crowd, to the mob! What a desecration of the libraries! What an absence of the 'law and order' we are so justly proud of. Instead of *regulations* discussed and elaborated by a dozen committees of civil servants inventing hundreds of formalities and obstacles to the use of books, they see to it that even *children* can make use of the rich collections; that readers can read publicly-owned books at home; they regard as the pride and glory of a public library, not the number of rarities it contains, the number of sixteenth-century editions or tenth-century manuscripts, but *the extent* to which books are distributed among *the people*, the number of new readers enrolled, the speed with which the demand for any book is met, the number of books issued to be read at home, the number of children attracted to reading and to the use of the library.... These queer prejudices are widespread in the Western States, and we must be glad that those who keep watch and ward over us protect us with care and circumspection from the influence of these prejudices, protect our rich public libraries from the mob, the hoi polloi!

I have before me the report of the New York Public Library for 1911. That year the Public Library in New York was moved from two old buildings to new premises erected by the city. The total number of books is now about two million. It so happened that the first book asked for when the reading-room opened its doors was in Russian. It was a work by N. Grot, *The Moral Ideals of Our Times*. The request for the book was handed in at eight minutes past nine in the morning. The book was delivered to the reader at nine fifteen.

In the course of the year the library was visited by 1,658,376 people. There were 246,950 readers using the reading-room and they took out 911,891 books.

This, however, is only a small part of the *book circulation* effected by the library. Only a few people can visit the library. The rational organisation of education work is measured by the number of books issued to be read at home, by the conveniences available to *the majority of the population*. In three boroughs of New York – Manhattan, Bronx and Richmond – the New York Public Library has *forty-two* branches and will soon have a forty-third (the total population of the three boroughs is almost three million). The aim that is constantly pursued is to have a branch of the Public Library within *three-quarters of a verst*, that is within ten minutes walk of the house of every inhabitant, the branch library being *the centre* of all kinds of institutions and establishments for public education.

Almost *eight million* (7,914,882) volumes were issued to readers at home, 400,000 more than in 1910. To each hundred members of the population of all ages and both sexes, 267 books were issued for reading at home in the course of the year. Each of the forty-two branch libraries not only provides for the use of reference books in the building and the issue of books to be read at home, but is also a place for evening lectures, for public meetings and for cultural entertainment. The New York Public Library contains about 15,000 books in Oriental languages, about 20,000 in Yiddish and about 16,000 in the Slav languages. In the main reading-room there are about 20,000 books standing on *open* shelves for general use. The New York Public Library has opened a special, central reading-room for children, and similar institutions are gradually being opened in all branches. The librarians do everything for the children's convenience and answer their questions. The number of books children took out to read at home was 2,859,888, slightly under three million (more than one-third of the total). The number of children visiting the reading-room was 1,120,915.

As far as losses are concerned – the New York Public Library assesses the number of books lost at 70–80–90 per 100,000 issued to be read at home.

Such is the way things are done in New York. And in Russia ?[11]

V. I. LENIN

PAGES FROM A DIARY

January 1923

The recent publication of the report on literacy among the population of Russia, based on the census of 1920 (*Literacy in Russia*, issued by the Central Statistical Board, Public Education Section, Moscow, 1922), is a very important event.

Below is a table from this report on the state of literacy among the population of Russia in 1897 and 1920.

Area	Literates per thousand males		Literates per thousand females		Literates per thousand population	
	1897	1920	1897	1920	1897	1920
1. European Russia	326	422	136	255	229	330
2. North Caucasus	241	357	56	215	150	291
3. Siberia (Western)	170	307	46	134	108	218
Overall average	318	409	131	244	223	319

At a time when we hold forth on proletarian culture and the relation in which it stands to bourgeois culture, facts and figures reveal that we are in a very bad way even as far as bourgeois culture is concerned. As might have been expected, it appears that we are still a very long way from attaining universal literacy, and that even compared with tsarist times (1897) our progress has been far too slow. This should serve as a stern warning and reproach to those who have been soaring in the empyreal heights of 'proletarian culture'. It shows what a vast amount of urgent spade-work we still have to do to reach the standard of an ordinary West-European civilised country. It also shows what a vast amount of work we have to do today to achieve, on the basis of our proletarian gains, anything like a real cultural standard.

We must not confine ourselves to this incontrovertible but too theoretical proposition. The very next time we revise our quarterly budget we must take this matter up in a practical way as well. In the first place, of course, we shall have to cut down on the expenditure of government departments other than the People's Commissariat of Education, and the sums thus released should be assigned for the latter's needs. In a year like the present, when we are relatively well supplied, we must not be chary of increasing the bread ration for school teachers.

Generally speaking, it cannot be said that the work now being done in public education is too narrow. Quite a lot is being done to get the old teachers out of their rut, to attract them to the new problems, to rouse their interest in new methods of education, and in such problems as religion.

But we are not doing the main thing. We are not doing anything – or doing far from enough – to raise the schoolteacher to the level that is absolutely essential if we want any culture at all, proletarian or even bourgeois. We must bear in mind the semi-Asiatic ignorance from which we have not yet extricated ourselves, and from which we cannot extricate ourselves without strenuous effort – although we have every opportunity to do so, because nowhere are the masses of the people so interested in real culture as they are in our country; nowhere are the problems of this culture tackled so thoroughly and consistently as they are in our country; in no other country is State power in the hands of the working class which, in its mass, is fully aware of the deficiencies, I shall not say of its culture, but of its literacy; nowhere is the working class so ready to make, and nowhere is it actually making, such sacrifices to improve its position in this respect as in our country.

Too little, far too little, is still being done by us to adjust our State budget to satisfy, as a first measure, the requirements of elementary public education. Even if we look at our People's Commissariat of Education we all too often find disgracefully inflated staffs in some State publishing establishment, which is contrary to the concept that the State's first concern should not be publishing houses but people; that the number of people able to read is greater, so that book publishing should have a wider political field in Russia. Owing to the old (and bad) habit, we are still devoting much more time and effort to technical questions, such as the question of book publishing, than to the general political question of literacy among the people. . . .[12]

KLARA ZETKIN

ILLITERACY AND SOCIALIST CONSTRUCTION

It was in 1907 ... that Rosa Luxemburg, who possessed an artist's eye for the characteristic, pointed Lenin out to me with the remark: 'Take a good look at him. That is Lenin. Look at the self-willed, stubborn head. A real Russian peasant's head with a few faintly Asiatic lines. That man will try to overturn mountains. Perhaps he will be crushed by them. But he will never yield.'

It was in the early autumn of 1920 that I first saw Lenin again after the outbreak of the Russian revolution. ...

I found Lenin's wife and sister at supper, which I was immediately and heartily asked to share. It was a simple meal, as the hard times demanded: tea, black bread, butter, cheese. Later the sister tried to find something 'sweet' for the 'guest of honour' and discovered a small jar of preserves. It was well known that the peasants provided 'their Ilyich' with gifts of white flour, bacon, eggs, fruit, etc.; but it was also well known that nothing remained in Lenin's household. Everything found its way to the hospitals and children's homes; Lenin's family held strictly to the principle of not living better than the others, that is, than the working masses. ...

Lenin found us three women discussing art and questions of education and instruction. I expressed my enthusiastic admiration for the titanic cultural work of the Bolsheviks, for the energy and activity of creative forces, which were opening up new channels for art and education. But I did not conceal my impression that there was a great deal that was uncertain, unclear, hesitating and experimental and together with the passionate desire for a new content, new forms, new ways of cultural life there were many artificial, cultural fashions after the Western model. Lenin immediately entered with great liveliness into the discussion:

'The awakening, the activity of forces which will create a new art and culture in Soviet Russia', he said, 'is good, very good.

The stormy rate of this development is understandable and useful. We must and shall make up for what has been neglected for centuries. The chaotic ferment, the feverish search for new solutions and new watchwords, the "Hosannah" for certain artistic and spiritual tendencies today, the "crucify them" tomorrow! – all that is unavoidable.

'The revolution is liberating all the forces which have been held back, and is driving them up from the depths to the surface. Let us take an example. Think of the pressure exercised on the development of our painting, sculpture and architecture by the fashions and moods of the tsarist court, as well as by the taste, the fancies of the aristocrats and the bourgeoisie. In a society based on private property the artist produces goods for the market – he needs buyers. Our revolution has lifted the pressure of this most prosaic state of affairs from the artists. It has made the Soviet State their protector and patron. Every artist, and everybody who wishes to, can claim the right to create freely according to his ideal, whether it turns out to be good or not. And so you have the ferment, the experiment, the chaos.

'But of course we are communists. We must not put our hands in our pockets and let chaos ferment as it pleases. We must consciously try to guide this development, to form and determine its results. . . .

'Why turn away from real beauty, and discard it for good and all . . . just because it is "old" ? Why worship the new as the god to be obeyed, just because it is "the new" ? That is nonsense, sheer nonsense. There is a great deal of conventional art hypocrisy in it too, and respect for the art fashions of the West. Of course, unconscious! We are good revolutionaries, but we feel obliged to point out that we stand at the "height of contemporary culture". I have the courage to show myself a "barbarian". I cannot value the works of expressionism, futurism, cubism, and other isms as the highest expressions of artistic genius. I don't understand them. They give me no pleasure. . . .'

. . . Lenin laughed heartily. 'Yes, dear Klara, we two are old. We must be satisfied with remaining young for a little longer in the revolution. We don't understand the new art any more, we just limp behind it.'

'But,' Lenin continued, 'our opinion on art is not important. Nor is it important what art gives to a few hundreds or even thousands out of a population as great as ours. Art belongs to the people. It must have its deepest roots in the broad mass of workers. It must be understood and loved by them. It must be rooted in and grow with their feelings, thoughts and desires. It must arouse and develop the artist in them. Are we to give cake and sugar to a minority when the mass of workers and peasants still lack black bread ? . . .'

'So that art may come to the people, and the people to art, we must first of all raise the general level of education and culture. And how is our country in that respect? You are amazed at the tremendous cultural work we have accomplished since the seizure of power. Without being boastful we can say that we have done much in this respect, very much. We have not only cut off heads, as the Mensheviks and their Kautskys in all countries accuse us of doing; we have also enlightened heads. Many heads. . . . We are confronted with the gigantic needs of the workers and peasants for education and culture, needs awakened and stimulated by us. . . . And we are a poor nation, a mendicant nation, whether we like it or not, the majority of the old people remain culturally the victims, the disinherited. . . .'

'While in Moscow today ten thousand – and perhaps tomorrow another ten thousand – are charmed by brilliant theatrical performances, millions are crying out to learn the art of spelling, of writing their names, are crying out for culture, are anxious to learn, for they are beginning to understand that the universe is ruled by natural laws, and not by the "Heavenly Father" and his witches and wizards.'

'Don't complain so bitterly of the illiteracy, Comrade Lenin', I interjected. 'To a certain extent it really helped forward the revolution. It prevented the mind of the workers and peasants from being stopped up and corrupted with bourgeois ideas and conceptions. Your propaganda and agitation is falling on virgin soil. It is easier to sow and to reap where you have not first of all had to uproot a whole forest.'

'Yes, that is true,' Lenin replied, 'but only within certain limits, or, more correctly, for a certain period of our struggle. . . .

Illiteracy is incompatible with the tasks of construction. As Marx said, it must be the task of the worker himself, and, I will add, of the peasant, to set himself free. Our Soviet society makes that possible. . . .'

'We are doing our very utmost to draw in new men and women into Soviet work and in this way to instruct them practically and theoretically. The need for administrative and constructive forces cannot be disguised. We are compelled to employ bureaucrats of the old style, and we are getting a future bureaucracy. I hate it heartily. Not the individual bureaucrat – he may be a capable rascal. But I hate the system. It paralyses and corrupts from above and below. And the most important weapon in overcoming and uprooting bureaucracy is the widest possible popular education and instruction. . . .'

'Do not let us forget that our workers and peasants are no Roman mob. They are not maintained by the State, they maintain the State by their work. . . . Our workers and peasants truly deserve more than circuses. They have the right to true, great art. So, before everything else, wide popular education and instruction. They are the cultural soil – assuming the bread is assured – on which a truly new, great art will grow up, a communist art, arranging its forms in accordance with its content.'[13]

13 or 14 November 1913

Dear A.M.,

Whatever are you doing? This is simply terrible, it really is!

Yesterday I read your reply in *Rech* to the 'howling' over Dostoevsky, and was preparing to rejoice, but today the liquidators' paper arrives, and *in it there is a paragraph of your article* which was not in *Rech*.

This paragraph runs as follows:

'And "god-seeking" should be for the time being' (only for the time being?) 'put aside – it is a useless occupation: it's no use seeking where there is nothing to be found. Unless you sow, you cannot reap. You have no god, you have not *yet*' (yet!) 'created him. Gods are not sought – *they are created*; people do not invent life, they create it.'

So it turns out that you are against 'god-seeking' only 'for the time being'!! It turns out that you are against god-seeking *only* in order to replace it by god-building!!

Well, isn't it horrible that such a thing should *appear* in your article?

God-seeking differs from god-building or god-creating or god-making, etc., no more than a yellow devil differs from a blue devil. To talk about god-seeking, not in order to declare against *all* devils and gods, against every ideological necrophily (all worship of divinity is necrophily – be it the cleanest, most ideal, not sought-out but built-up divinity, it's all the same), but to prefer a blue devil to a yellow one is a hundred times worse than not saying anything about it at all.

In the freest countries, in countries where it is *quite* out of place to appeal 'to democracy, to the people, to public opinion and science', in such countries (America, Switzerland, and so forth) particular zeal is applied to render the people and the workers obtuse with just this very idea of a clean, spiritual, built-up god. Just because any religious idea, any idea of any god at all, any flirtation even with a god, is the most inexpressible foulness tolerantly (and often even favourably) accepted by the *democratic* bourgeoisie – for that very reason it is the most dangerous foulness, the most shameful 'infection'. A million *physical* sins, dirty tricks, acts of violence and pests are much more easily discovered by the crowd, and therefore are much less dangerous than the *subtle*, spiritual idea of god, dressed up in the most attractive 'ideological' costumes. The Catholic priest corrupting young girls (about whom I have just read by chance in a German newspaper) is *much less* dangerous, precisely to 'democracy', than a priest without his robes, a priest without crude religion, an ideologically equipped and democratic priest preaching the creation and the invention of a god. For it is *easy* to expose, condemn and expel the first priest, while the second *cannot* be expelled so simply; to expose the latter is a thousand times more difficult, and not a single 'frail and pitifully wavering' philistine will agree to 'condemn' him.

And you, knowing the 'frailty and pitiful wavering' of the Russian (Why Russian? Is the Italian any better??) *philistine* soul, confuse that soul with the sweetest of poisons, most effectively disguised in lollipops and all kinds of gaily-coloured wrappings!!

Really, it is terrible.

'Enough of self-humiliation, which is our substitute for self-criticism.'

And isn't god-building the *worst* form of self-humiliation? Everyone who sets about building up a *god*, or who even merely tolerates such activity, *humiliates* himself in the worst possible way, because instead of 'deeds' he is *actually* engaged in self-contemplation, self-admiration and, moreover, such a man 'contemplates' the dirtiest, most stupid, most slavish features or traits of his 'ego', defied by god-building.

From the point of view, not of the individual, but of society, *all* god-building is precisely the fond *self-deception* of the thick-witted philistine, the frail man in the street, the dreamy 'self-humiliation' of the vulgar petty bourgeois, 'exhausted and in despair' (as you condescended to say very truly about the *soul*: only you should have said, not 'the Russian', but the *petty-bourgeois*, for the Jewish, the Italian, the English varieties are all *one and the same devil*; stinking philistinism everywhere is equally disgusting – but 'democratic philistinism', engaged in ideological necrophily, is particularly disgusting).

Reading your article over and over again, and *trying to*

discover where this *slip* of your tongue could come from, I am at a loss. What does it mean? A relic of the 'Confession', which *you yourself* did not approve?? Or its echo??

Or something different: for example, an unsuccessful attempt to *bend back* to the viewpoint of *democracy in general*, instead of the viewpoint of the proletariat? Perhaps it was in order to talk with 'democracy in general' that you decided (excuse the expression) to indulge in baby-talk? Perhaps it was 'for a popular exposition to the *philistines*' that you decided to accept for a moment *their*, the philistines', prejudices??

But then that is a *wrong* approach, in all senses and in all respects! ...

Why do you do this?

It's damnably disappointing.

Yours,

V.I.

... P.P.S. Get as good *medical* treatment as you can, please, so that you can travel in the winter *without colds*. (It's dangerous in the winter.)

Yours,

V. Ulyanov[14]

31 July 1919

Dear Alexei Maximych,

The more I read over your letter, and the more I think of the connection between its conclusions and what it sets forth (and what you described at our meetings), the more I arrive at the conviction that the letter, and your conclusions, and all your impressions, are quite sick.

Petrograd has been one of the sickest places in recent times. This is quite understandable, since its population has suffered most of all, the workers have given up more of their best forces than anyone else, the food shortage is grave, and the military danger too. Obviously your nerves can't stand it. That is not surprising. Yet you won't listen when you are told that you ought to change your abode, because to let oneself flog the nerves to a state of sickness is very unwise, unwise even from the plain common-sense point of view, not to speak of other points of view.

Just as in your conversations, there is in your letter a sum of sick impressions, leading you to sick conclusions.

You begin with dysentery and cholera, and immediately a kind of sick resentment comes over you: 'fraternity, equality'. Unconscious, but the result is something like communism being responsible for the privations, poverty and diseases of a besieged city!!

Then follow some bitter witticisms, which I don't understand, against 'hoarding' literature. . . . And the conclusion that 'wretched remnants of sensible workers' say that they have been 'sold into captivity to the moujik'.

This makes absolutely no sense. Is it Kalinin who is being accused of selling the workers to the moujik? That's what it amounts to.

This might be invented by workers who are either quite green, stupid, with a 'left' phrase instead of a brain, or else by the 'remnants of the aristocracy' who had a splendid ability to distort everything, a splendid gift for picking on every trifle to vent their frenzied hatred of Soviet power. You yourself mention these remnants at the same point in your letter. Their state of mind is having an unhealthy influence on you.

You write that you see 'people of the most varied sections of society'. It's one thing to see them, another thing to be in daily contact with them, in all aspects of life. Your experience comes mainly from the 'remnants' – if only by virtue of your profession, which obliges you to 'receive' dozens of embittered bourgeois intellectuals, and also by virtue of your general circumstances.

As though the 'remnants' cherish 'something bordering on sympathy for Soviet power', while 'the majority of the workers' produce thieves, 'communists' who have jumped on the bandwagon, etc! And you talk yourself into the 'conclusion' that a revolution cannot be made with the help of thieves, cannot be made without the intelligentsia.

This is a completely sick psychology, acutely aggravated in the environment of embittered bourgeois intellectuals.

Everything is being done to draw the intelligentsia (the nonwhiteguard intelligentsia) into the struggle against the thieves. And *month by month* the Soviet Republic acquires a *growing* percentage of bourgeois intellectuals who are *sincerely* helping the workers and peasants, not merely grumbling and spitting fury. This cannot be 'seen' in Petrograd, because Petrograd is a city with an exceptionally large number of bourgeois people (and 'intelligentsia') who have lost their place in life (and their heads), but for all Russia this is an unquestionable fact.

In Petrograd, or from Petrograd, one can only become convinced of this if one is exceptionally well informed *politically* and has a specially wide political experience. This you haven't got. And you are engaged, not in politics and not in observing the *work* of political construction, but in a particular profession, which surrounds you with embittered bourgeois intellectuals, who have understood nothing, forgotten nothing, learnt nothing and *at best* – a very rare best – have lost their bearings, are in despair, moaning, repeating old prejudices, have been frightened to death or are frightening themselves to death.

If you want to *observe*, you must observe from below, where it is possible to perceive the work of building a new life, in a workers' settlement in the provinces or in the countryside. There one does not have to make a political summing-up of extremely complex data, there one need only observe. Instead of this, you have put yourself in the position of a professional editor of translations, etc., a position in which it is impossible to observe the new building of a new life, a position in which all your strength is frittered away on the sick grumbling of a sick intelligentsia, on observing the 'former' capital in conditions of desperate military peril and acute privations.

You have put yourself in a position in which you *cannot* directly observe the new features in the life of the workers and peasants, that is, nine-tenths of the population of Russia; in which you are compelled to observe the fragments of life of a former capital, from where the flower of the workers has gone to the fronts and to the countryside, and where there remain a disproportionately large number of intellectuals without a place in life and without jobs, who *specially* '*besiege*' you. Counsels to go away you stubbornly reject.

Quite understandably, you have reduced yourself to a condition of sickness; you write that you find life not only hard, but also 'extremely revolting'!!! I should say so! At such a time, to chain oneself to the sickest of places as an editor of translated literature (a most suitable occupation for observing people, for an artist!). As the artist, you *cannot* see and study anything there that is new – in the army, in the countryside, in the factory. You have deprived yourself of any opportunity of doing what would satisfy the artist: in Petrograd a politician can work, but you are not a politician. Today it's windows being broken for no reason at all; tomorrow it will be shots and screams from prison, then snatches of oratory by the most weary of the non-workers who have remained in Petrograd, then millions of impressions from the intelligentsia, the intelligentsia of a capital which is no longer a capital, then hundreds of complaints from those who have been wronged, *inability* to see any building of the new life in the time left to you after editing . . . how not to reduce oneself to a state in which it is extremely revolting to go on living?

The country is feverishly struggling against the bourgeoisie of the whole world which takes a frenzied revenge for its overthrow. Naturally, for the creation of the first Soviet Republic – first blows *from everywhere*. Naturally. Here one must live either as an active politician or (if one's heart is not in politics) as an artist, observe how people are building life anew somewhere, but not in the capital which is the centre of furious attack, of a furious struggle against conspiracies, of the furious anger of the capital's intelligentsia – somewhere in the countryside, or in a provincial factory (or at the front). There it is easy, merely by observing, to distinguish the decomposition of the old from the first shoots of the new.

Life has become revolting, the 'divergence' from communism 'is deepening'. Where the divergence lies, it is impossible to tell. Not a shadow of an indication whether it is in politics or in ideas. There is a divergence of *mood* – between people who are engaged in politics or absorbed in a struggle of the most furious kind and the mood of a man who has artificially driven himself into a situation where he can't observe the new life, while his impressions of the decay of a vast bourgeois capital are getting the better of him.

I have expressed my thoughts to you frankly on the subject of your letter. In my conversations (with you) I have long been approaching the same ideas, but your letter gave shape and conclusion, it rounded off the sum total of the impressions I have gained from these conversations. I don't want to thrust my advice on you, but I cannot help saying: change your circumstances radically, your environment, your abode, your occupation – otherwise life may disgust you for good.

All the best.

Yours,

Lenin[15]

15 September 1919

Dear Alexei Maximych,

I received Tonkov, but even before I had received him and before your letter, we had decided in the Central Committee to appoint Kamenev and Bukharin to check on the arrests of the bourgeois intellectuals of the near-Cadet type and to see which of them can be released; for it is clear to us that mistakes were also made here.

It is also clear that, on the whole, the arrest of the Cadet (and near-Cadet) crowd was a correct and necessary measure.

When I read your frank opinion on this matter, I recall a phrase of yours which struck me particularly during our conversations (in London, Capri, and afterwards):

'We artists are an irresponsible lot.'

Why do you speak in such an angry, ill-tempered manner? Just because some tens (albeit even some hundreds) of Cadet and near-Cadet little gentlemen will spend a few days in prison in order to *forestall conspiracies*, similar to that *of the Red Hill Fort*, conspiracies which threaten the lives of *tens* of thousands of workers and peasants.

Think only, what calamity, what injustice! A few days or even weeks of prison for intellectuals in order to prevent the slaughter of tens of thousands of workers and peasants!

'Artists are an irresponsible lot!'

To identify the 'intellectual forces' of the nation with the 'forces' of the bourgeois members of the intelligentsia is wrong.

As an example I shall take Korolenko: not long ago I read his pamphlet, written in August 1917, on *War, Fatherland, and Mankind*. Korolenko is one of the best 'near-Cadets' – he is nearly a Menshevik. And what a dull, vile, disgusting defence of the imperialist war, covered up with sugared phrases! Pitiable bourgeois enslaved by bourgeois prejudices! For such men, the imperialist war with 10,000,000 killed is a thing worthy of support . . . and the death of hundreds of thousands in the *just* civil war against landlords and capitalists provokes oh! and ah!, sighing and hysterics.

No. It is not a sin to keep such 'talents' in prison for a few weeks, if this *has* to be done in order to prevent conspiracies (of the Red Hill kind) and a massacre of tens of thousands. We have uncovered the plots of Cadets and 'near-Cadets', And we *know* that the near-Cadet professors constantly give the conspirators their *assistance*. This is a fact.

The intellectual forces of the workers and peasants grow and get stronger in the struggle against the bourgeoisie and its accomplices, the petty intelligentsia, the lackeys of capitalism, who consider themselves the brain of the nation. In fact it is not the brain, but m . . .

To the 'intellectual forces' who wish to educate the nation (and not to fawn on capital) we pay an *above* average salary. This is a fact. We take great care of them. This is a fact. Tens of thousands of officers serve us in the Red Army despite hundreds of traitors. This is a fact.

As to the 'understanding' of your moods – yes, I understand them (once you were wondering whether I shall understand you). More than once, in Capri and later on, I told you: you allow yourself to be surrounded by the worst elements of the bourgeois intelligentsia and you succumb to its whimperings. You hear, and you listen to the lamentations of hundreds of intellectuals about the 'terrible' arrest for a few weeks; but you do not hear and you do not listen to the voice of the masses, to the millions, to the workers and peasants threatened by Denikin, Kolchak, Lyazonov, Rodzianko, and Red Hill conspirators. I quite understand, I fully, fully understand that in this way one might also work oneself not only into 'the reds-as-much-as-the-whites are the enemies of the nation' (those who fight to overthrow capitalists and landlords are as much an enemy of the nation as are the landlords and the capitalists) but also into belief in the good god or in tsar-*batiushka*;* I fully understand.

Yes, yes, you'll perish if you do not wrench yourself out of this bourgeois-intelligentsia set-up! From the bottom of my heart I wish that you do this quickly.

Best greetings!

Lenin

P.S. Of course, you write nothing. To waste oneself on the whining of rotting intellectuals and not to write – for an artist isn't this a ruin, isn't this a shame ?[16]

On 1 August 1919, a fortnight before this letter to Gorky was written, the following message 'all in code' was despatched to:

Rozengolts
Revolutionary Military Council 7

Has every measure been taken to hold Petrograd at all costs ? We are pushing ahead with the promised reinforcements, but it will take time for them to arrive. Make an exceptional effort.

Lenin[17]

---

* *batiushka*: Little Father.

A. V. LUNACHARSKY

A TALK WITH GORKY

(Lunacharsky was present at a conversation in 1919 between Vladimir Ilyich and A. M. Gorky. Gorky complained about searches and arrests among some members of the Petrograd intelligentsia.)

'But they are the same people', went on the writer, 'who assisted you personally, hid you in their homes, etc.'

Smiling, Vladimir Ilyich answered:

'Yes, of course they are excellent, good people and that is precisely why their homes have to be searched. Precisely because of this one has sometimes *à contre coeur* to arrest them. Of course they are excellent and good, of course their sympathy goes always to the oppressed, of course they are always against persecution. And what do they see now around them? The persecutor – our Cheka; the oppressed – the Cadets and the S.R.s who flee from it. Obviously, their duty, as they conceive it, tells them to ally themselves with the Cadets and the S.R.s against us. And we must catch active counter-revolutionaries and render them harmless. The rest is clear.'

And Vladimir Ilyich laughed, quite without malice. . . .[18]

WHAT TO DO WITH COUNTER-REVOLUTIONARY WRITERS: LETTER TO F. E. DZERZHINSKY

19 May 1922

Comrade Dzerzhinsky,

On the question of banishing abroad the writers and professors who help the counter-revolution.

This should be prepared more thoroughly. Without preparation we shall do something foolish. Please, discuss preparatory measures.

Call Messing, Mantzev and some other people to a meeting in Moscow.

Make the Politbureau members devote two to three hours a week for looking through a number of publications and books, checking whether this has been done, *demanding opinions in writing*, and securing the despatch to Moscow of all non-communist publications without delay.

Add to this the opinion of a number of communist writers (Steklov's, Olminsky's, Skvortsev's, Bukharin's, etc.).

Collect *systematic* information about the political record, work and literary activity of the professors and writers.

Assign all this to a sensible, educated and scrupulous man at the G.P.U.

My opinion of the two Petrograd publications:

Novaya Rossiya, Nr 2. Closed down by the Petrograd comrades.

Hasn't it been closed too soon? It should be circulated among *Politbureau* members and judged more attentively. Who is *Lezhnev*, its editor? Is he from *Dyen*? Couldn't information about him be collected? Of course, *not all* who work on that journal are candidates for dispatch abroad.

Quite another matter is the Petrograd journal *Economist* of the eleventh department of the Russian Technical Society. This, to my mind, is clearly a centre of white-guardists. In Nr 3 (*only* Nr 3!!! This *nota bene*!) there is on the cover a list of contributors. These, I think are *nearly all* most legitimate candidates for exile abroad.

They are all openly counter-revolutionaries, accomplices of

the *Entente*, an organisation of its servants and spies and corrupters of the student youth. Arrangements should be made to have these 'military spies' seized and constantly and systematically caught and dispatched abroad.

I am asking that this should be, secretly and without making any copies, shown to the members of the *Politbureau, returned to you and to me*, and that I should be informed about their reaction and your conclusion.

Lenin[19]

LENIN AT AN EXHIBITION

Lenin had, throughout his life, very little time to devote to anything like a systematic study of art, and always considered himself ignorant on these matters; and since he hated all dilettantism which was so alien to his nature, he disliked to express himself on the subject of arts. Nonetheless, he had very definite tastes: he liked Russian classics, realism in literature and painting, etc.

Once, in 1905, during the first revolution, Lenin had to spend the night in the flat of Comrade D. I. Leshchenko who had a large collection of Knackfuss editions of the world's great artists. Next morning Vladimir Ilyich said to me: 'What a fascinating field is the history of art. How much work there is in it for a Marxist! I could not fall asleep till the morning, I looked through one book after another. What a pity that I never had nor will I ever have time to devote to art.' I remember these words very clearly.

After the revolution we had several meetings in connection with various art competitions. Once, I remember, he called me in and together with Kamenev we went to an exhibition of projects for a monument which had to replace that of Alexander III which had been pulled down from its gorgeous plinth near the Church of Christ the Saviour. Vladimir Ilyich looked at all the projects very critically. He did not like any of them. Especially amazed he stood in front of a monument done in a futuristic manner, but, when asked about his views, he said: 'I don't understand anything in this; ask Lunacharsky.' When I told him that I did not see any worthy design there, he was very glad and said: 'And I thought you'd put up some futuristic monstrosity.'

Another time the matter concerned a monument to Karl Marx. The well-known sculptor M. was particularly insistent. He presented a large project: 'Karl Marx Standing on Four Elephants'. Such unexpected motif seemed to us all, and to Vladimir Ilyich, rather odd. The artist began to alter his design, remade it three times, adamantly refusing to acknowledge his defeat at the competition. When the jury, over which I presided, finally rejected his project and decided on the one presented by a team of artists headed by Alyeshin, the sculptor M. burst into Vladimir Ilyich's office and complained to him. Vladimir Ilyich took his complaint to heart, and rang me up to have a new jury convened. He said he would come to see the Alyeshin project and M's design. He still liked the Alyeshin design and rejected the one presented by M.

That same year, on May Day, Alyeshin's group put up a small-scale model on the place where the monument to Marx was to be erected. Vladimir Ilyich went there especially to see it. He walked around the model several times, asked how big the monument was to be and was pleased with it. 'Anatol Vassilyevich,' he said to me however, 'be sure to tell the artist that the head has to be lifelike, so one would have the same impression of Karl Marx which one has from his better portraits, because there does not seem to be much likeness here.'[20]

6 May 1921

Aren't you ashamed to vote for printing 5,000 copies of Mayakovsky's '150,000,000'?

It is nonsense, stupidity, double-dyed stupidity and affectation.

I believe such things should be published one time out of ten, and *not more than 1,500 copies*, for libraries and cranks.

As for Lunacharsky, he should be flogged for his futurism.

Lenin[21]

6 May 1921

Comrade Pokrovsky,

Again and again I am asking you to help in the struggle against futurism, etc.

1. Lunacharsky made the Collegium (oho!) pass the publication of Mayakovsky's '150,000,000'.

Cannot this be stopped? It should be stopped. Let's agree to publish these futurists twice a year and *in not more than 1,500 copies*.

2. Kiselis, who is said to be a 'realist' artist, was again squeezed out by Lunacharsky who promoted the futurist directly and *indirectly*.

Can't any reliable *anti*-futurist be found?

Lenin[22]

V. I. LENIN

OBLOMOV STILL LIVES - ON MAYAKOVSKY

6 March 1922

'... Yesterday I happened to read in *Izvestia* a political poem by Mayakovsky ['Incessant Meeting Sitters']. I am not an admirer of his poetical talent, although I admit that I am not a competent judge. But I have not for a long time read anything on politics and administration with so much pleasure as I read this. In his poem he derides this meeting habit, and taunts the communists with incessant meetings. I am not sure about the poetry; but as for the politics, I vouch for their absolute correctness. We are indeed in a position, and it must be said that it is a very absurd position, of people sitting endlessly at meetings, setting up commissions and drawing up plans without end. There was a character who typified Russian life - Oblomov. He was always lolling on his bed and mentally drawing up schemes. That was a long time ago. Russia has experienced three revolutions, but the Oblomovs have survived, for there were Oblomovs not only among the landowners, but also among the peasants; not only among the peasants but among the intellectuals, and not only among the intellectuals, but also among the workers and communists. It is enough to watch us at our meetings, at our work on commissions, to be able to say that *old Oblomov still lives; and it will be necessary to give him a good washing and cleaning, a good rubbing and scouring to make a man of him.* In this respect we must have no illusions about our position. We have not imitated any of those who write the word 'revolution' with a capital R, as the Social-Revolutionaries do. But we can quote the words of Marx that many foolish things are done during a revolution, perhaps more than at any other time. We revolutionaries must learn to regard these foolish acts dispassionately and fearlessly.[23]

A VISIT TO A STUDENTS' HOSTEL

In the period between 1920 and 1922 I had a chance to see Lenin quite often as he and Nadezhda Krupskaya, after my mother's death, took my sister, my brother and myself under their care. . . .

One day at the end of February 1921, I went to visit Nadezhda Konstantinovna. We were sitting in her room in the Kremlin flat and chatting when Vladimir Ilyich came in. As was his habit, while talking he was pacing quickly up and down the room. That evening, I remember, he was lively and cheerful, and inquired how I lived and worked. Then he asked about my sister Varvara who was still a student at the Higher Art-Technical Institute and lived in the students' hostel. Vladimir Ilyich started asking all sorts of detailed questions about con-ditions of students' life: was it warm in the hostel? was there enough food? how did the work go? Relying on what my sister told me, I assured him that the students' conditions were good and that she had all she needed. Vladimir Ilyich listened to me with some scepticism and then, unexpectedly, suggested to Nadezhda Konstantinovna: 'Nadya, let's go and visit Varya – we shall see how the young are living.' It was already 11 p.m. but Nadezhda agreed. They took me with them. In the car Vladimir Ilyich went on teasing me: 'We shall check, we shall check whether you tell the truth! . . .'

We had to cross a dark courtyard and go up slippery ice-coated stairs. Vladimir Ilyich went forward together with the guard and kept on striking one match after another as it was pitch dark. 'Well, well, nice beginning', I said to myself horrified, helping Nadezhda Konstantinovna up. However, all my fears were dispersed when we entered the hall.

The youngsters met Lenin enthusiastically. He was immedi-ately surrounded and greeted gaily. The news about his arrival spread. Students rushed in from all sides and he found himself in the middle of a tight circle. He was very lively, good-humoured

* Little Inessa was the daughter of Inessa Armand.

and glad to meet them all. We went to look at the dormitories. Lenin even felt the beds, or rather the rough wooden planks which served as beds. There was hardly any furniture in the hostel, but the walls were decorated with slogans, drawings and a wall newspaper.

Vladimir Ilyich noticed the drawing of a locomotive with some original 'dynamic' lines. The author of the drawing began to assure us that that was how real locomotives should be painted: from his words one could only conclude that this kind of painting was supposed to affect the speed of the engine. This amused Lenin greatly.

Then Vladimir Ilyich turned towards a slogan, displayed on the wall, taken from a poem by Mayakovsky:

'We shall toss ferro-concrete into the sky.' Lenin, laughing, protested: 'Why into the sky? We need it on the earth.'

Vladimir Ilyich behaved with such simplicity and cheerfulness that soon a free and easy debate was in progress. The talk was about painting, about literature, and about the life and work of young artists. Unfortunately, much of this talk has slipped from my memory but I shall recall some moments.

The discussion started, of course, from the topic which most of all preoccupied young artists – the question of figurative art and above all figurative painting. All agreed on one thing: all stressed that art must keep in step with the revolution, must be politically sharp-edged, must 'go out of the museums into the street' and mobilise the masses for revolutionary struggle. This attitude was hotly maintained by all. But how to achieve this aim, how should art 'keep in step with the revolution' – to this question everybody had a different answer: many vehemently defended the futurists, some denounced easel painting.

Lenin liked this fervour and directness of youth, this contempt for routine and the passionate desire to serve the revolution. But from all that was said with so much fire, it was clear that nobody had a correct understanding of the future development of art. Lenin argued, defending realist painting, though to argue against two dozen people who talk all together, excitedly and interrupting each other, was not easy.

There was much talk about Mayakovsky. It started by enthusiastic remarks about the famous posters of Mayakovsky in the windows of Rosta. Vladimir Ilyich willingly admitted their great revolutionary significance. Then we spoke about Mayakovsky's poetry in general. It was obvious that Lenin enjoyed the enthusiastic way in which the young spoke about their beloved poet and about the revolutionary spirit of his verse. However there was much disagreement, as it turned out that there were many worshippers of futurism in poetry.

At the end, tired by the debate, he declared jokingly that he would make a special study of futurism in painting and poetry, that he would study the literature on this subject and then would come again and certainly be able to hold his own against all the disputants.

Then he asked whether they read Russian classical literature. What transpired was that they knew it only slightly and that many rejected it as 'left over from the old regime'. Lenin remarked that one should know and value the best in Russian pre-revolutionary literature. He himself, he said, liked Pushkin and held Nekrasov in high esteem, and added: 'You see, a whole generation of revolutionaries learned from Nekrasov.'

Of course, Lenin expressed his opinions not in the form of a speech or lecture. But throughout the discussion, in his answers and questions and in his remarks his view on the necessity of a critical assimilation of all that was best in the culture of the past became obvious. On this and not on some void should our new Soviet culture be built.

The talk then turned to the subject of students' existence. The particular section of the students' hostel we were visiting was run as a commune whose members belonged either to the party – or to the Communist Youth. Vladimir Ilyich inquired why they considered themselves a commune, how they ran their home, how they organised different tasks such as cleaning, etc.

Then he asked the students whether they had enough to eat and whether their rations were adequate. 'Everything is well, Vladimir Ilyich', came a friendly answer. 'At the most we are left without bread for the last four days of the month.' This kind of statement amused Lenin.

Lenin also wanted to know all about their academic and social work. Among other things, he asked whether they stayed up late at night. It turned out that not only do they stay up late, but that often they spent whole nights arguing about art, about their future education, and so on. Lenin got cross and started chiding them: 'You work hard,' he said, 'you feed yourselves badly, and on top of this you do not sleep. Nothing will come of you. You'll waste your strength and you'll be good for nothing, while it is your duty to "protect State property". I shall see to it that your lights are turned off for the night', he added.

Finally, the students invited Vladimir Ilyich and Nadezhda Konstantinovna to a meal. Nearly a whole month's ration was put on the table. But Vladimir Ilyich was tired and declined the invitation. Nadezhda Konstantinovna had at least to taste the gruel so as not to offend the hosts.

It was time to go, it was getting late. The students did not see the visitors off: it would be wrong to attract attention. Times were very troubled.

On our way back Vladimir Ilyich seemed thoughtful and silent. From the short 'Yes, yes' which he murmured from time to time in a special voice, one could feel that his mind was still on the recent meeting with the young and that he was preoccupied.

He never shared with me his impressions of the meeting, but I heard from Nadezhda Konstantinovna that when he met the Commissar of Education, Lunacharsky, he said reproachfully: 'Your youth is excellent, excellent, but whatever are you teaching them!'[24]

I

S. SENKIN

Somebody brought the drawing I made for the volume in memory of Kropotkin. Vladimir Ilyich grinned, glanced at the picture, then at me, and asked 'What does it represent?'

I tried as eloquently as I could to explain that the drawing was not supposed to represent anything in particular, that it was only old painters who deluded themselves and others, when they maintained that in their work they were able to represent something – nobody was able to do any such thing! As to us, we were now learning and our task was to link art with politics.

Vladimir took time to recover his breath, then threw a brief question at me:

'I see, and how do you link art with politics?'

He was examining the drawing from all sides as if trying to find this 'link'.

'Well, Vladimir Ilyich, we are not as yet capable of doing this, but we shall achieve it. For the time being we are preparing ourselves. Here we are analysing all the basic elements in order to learn how to gain control. . . .'

I felt that I could not express myself in two or three sentences and I began to get confused. Vladimir Ilyich came to my rescue:

'Well, I see I still have to study certain things; after I have done that I shall come back, especially for a debate with you.'[25]

II

M. GARLOVSKY

The young [students] belonged to the *avante-garde* and naturally approved of constructivism only. Among them there was one detested artist whom we all contemptuously called the dauber. But he remained undeterred and went on with his realistic pictures. It was just his work which gave Lenin pleasure. 'This, you see, is clear to me', he said. 'I understand this, so do you, and so do the workers and everybody else. But explain to me what do I see in your pictures? On all these human faces [painted by you] I cannot find either eyes or noses ?'[26]

III

M. GARLOVSKY

Lenin was talking gently, with a slightly ironic smile, sometimes with fatherly sternness, and he listened to us sympathetically.

'I understand Pushkin, and I value him highly; I value Nekrasov. But Mayakovsky! – excuse me I just do not understand him.'

'How many times have I told you, Volodya, that you should get Mayakovsky's books', laughed Nadezhda Konstantinovna. 'You would understand him too. You just cannot get down to this.'

Lenin got hold of a book written by the UNOVIS group and was informed that UNOVIS stands for *Utverditeli Novovo Iskusstva* or Consolidators of New Art. Lenin laughed: 'Well, think only, comrades, what does it look like U-NO-VIS. Who would understand this ?' The students were fidgeting: 'Vladimir Ilyich, and SOVNARKOM* – is this intelligible? Is it? What does it look like: SOV-NAR-KOM?'

You are right, comrades. SOV-NAR-KOM is not intelligible either. One should not introduce into literature these abbreviated titles. They came about under quite exceptional circumstances, and that is the only reason why we have to put up with them.

The chatter went on . . . Lenin promised to visit the students again. . . .[27]

IV

N. ALTMAN

Clearly someone must have told Lenin that I was a futurist so he asked me straightway whether I intended to make his bust in a 'futuristic style!' I said I wanted to portray him just as he was and that the aim determined the approach to my work. Then he asked me to show him some examples of 'futuristic' art. He

* Council of the People's Commissars.

looked and said: 'I understand nothing – for this one has to be a specialist!'

I showed him also a photograph of my bust of Lunacharsky. Lenin found that there was something unfamiliar in the expression of Lunacharsky's eyes. I remarked that the pince-nez which one was so accustomed to seeing on his face was not there. 'But then, how do you put a pince-nez on a sculpture?' Lenin asked.

On another occasion Lenin wanted to know how much I worked: the normal amount of hours? above or below the usual norm?[28]

V

Y. YAKOVLEV

. . . I would like to formulate briefly Comrade Lenin's views on the question of proletarian culture. I had some five conversations with him on the subject. The essence of his argument was this: he was against treating the proletarian culture as if it were a kind of laboratory. He considered dangerous the mere thought that proletarian culture might be produced as if in an incubator. *Proletkult* was such a hot house, such an incubator.

Proletarian culture can come into being only on the foundations of universal literacy in conditions of Soviet power, maintained Lenin. When, as a result of Soviet rule we shall have millions of educated people – now we only have very, very few of them – then there will really come into being a new type of culture and a new type of literature. It is essential that in our Soviet State the best achievements of bourgeois culture should become accessible to the masses. When millions make these achievements their own, then a base will exist on which true culture, not of a bourgeois character, will just begin to grow. This is why Lenin used to say to the workers: 'Learn, acquaint yourselves with bourgeois culture; don't let yourselves be deluded by tales that somewhere, in some institution whatever its name, there has grown the tree of proletarian culture. . . .'

Those who think in terms of hot-houses and incubators

don't understand anything about the processes of birth. For Comrade Lenin it was extremely characteristic that he had, at the time, suggested the closing down, simultaneously, of the *Bolshoi Theatre* and the *Proletkult* [organisation], treating them both as inessential.[29]

A. V. LUNACHARSKY

MUSEUMS AND EXPERIMENTING YOUTH

Once in a private conversation I asked Lenin: 'Wouldn't you allocate some money to support our experimental theatres – they are revolutionary and new.'

'It would be better', answered Lenin, 'if in these hungry times the experimental theatres supported themselves by their own enthusiasm. It is absolutely essential to make all efforts in order to prevent the pillars of our culture from crumbling to pieces – if this were to happen, the proletariat would never forgive us.'

Lenin maintained that, in the first instance, we must ensure that our museums containing great treasures, should not disintegrate and that our prominent experts-curators did not starve and did not run abroad, away from us. He thought we would be guilty of a minor sin only if we still failed to give priority to our experimenting youth.[30]

G. M. KZHIZHANOVSKY

ON DOSTOEVSKY

When Vladimir Ilyich asked that at the Council of the People's
Commissars a small library should be set up, he gave a list of
authors whose books should be included: Pushkin, Lermontov,
Gogol, Goncharov, Dostoevsky, Maykov, Nekrasov, Leskov,
L. N. Tolstoy, Griboyedov, Gleb Uspensky, S. T. Aksakov,
Saltykov-Shchedryn, Levitov, Koltsov, Tiutchev, Grigorovich,
Turgenev, Pomyalovsky, Fet, Apukhtin, A. K. Tolstoy,
Chekhov, Zlatovratsky, Kozma, Prutkov, Nadson, Dobro-
lyubov. . . .

In Lenin's office in the Council of the People's Commissars,
on a bookshelf by the table, and very often right on the table,
one could see the slim volume of Tiutchev, whose poetry Lenin
scanned and read again and again. . . . Lenin supported Gorky
who protested when the bourgeois newspapers began a reactionary demonstration on the occasion of a theatre performance of Dostoevsky's *The Possessed*. He flayed mercilessly the
reactionary tendencies of Dostoevsky's writings. In his letter to
Inessa Armand he sharply criticised the decadent and slan-
derous novel of Vinnichenko, *Fathers' Testaments*, and showed
that the main defect of this novel consisted in this that it was
'. . . an extremely bad imitation of what was extremely bad in
Dostoevsky'. At the same time Vladimir Ilyich stressed more
than once that Dostoevsky was indeed a genius of a writer, who
observed the sickness of contemporary society, that he was full
of contradictions and failings, and yet he was excellent in
providing many vivid images of reality.

Although Lenin's attitude to *The Possessed* was very negative,
he used to remark that the novel reflected events connected not
only with the activities of Nechayev, but also with those of
Bakunin. When Dostoevsky was engaged in writing *The
Possessed*, Marx and Engels were conducting an intense
struggle against Bakunin. It was a matter for the critics to
analyse what in the novel referred to Bakunin and what to
Nechayev.

On the whole, Vladimir Ilyich greatly valued Dostoevsky's talent. When Dostoevsky was mentioned, he used to remark:

'Don't forget that Dostoevsky was condemned to death, that he was subjected to barbaric degradations and only later was it announced that Nicholas I showed him 'mercy' by commuting his death sentence to that of penal servitude.'

The Notes from the House of the Dead, said Vladimir Ilyich, 'constitutes an unsurpassed achievement of Russian and world literature, because it so remarkably describes not only the Siberian penal colony, but also the House of the Dead in which the whole Russian people lived under the tsars of the House of the Romanovs.'

Vladimir Ilyich attentively studied the literature of the Narodniks. Severely criticising the Narodniks' principles and fighting a life and death struggle against Mikhailovsky, V. Vorontzov and other theoreticians of the Narodnik movement, he nevertheless recognised the great importance of such writers as Gleb Uspensky. . . . He was fascinated by Uspensky's stories of the life of workers and poor peasants, and stressed that this kind of literature should reach the masses and should be as widely distributed as possible.[31]

V. D. BONCH-BRUEVICH

AGAINST BUREAUCRATIC STYLE

When Vladimir Ilyich was writing or formulating a decree or an announcement meant for the broad masses, he always remembered, and demanded that others should remember, the importance of clarity, and precision. He was always approving of efforts at popularisation, but was an enemy of vulgarisation. When someone produced a piece of writing which was somewhat obscure, he used to ask: 'Are you really unable to express your thoughts in Russian in such a way that they should be accessible to all? Russian is a very rich language. If you do not write clearly, you, and not the language, are at fault.' He demanded from everybody – and the more responsible the comrade, the stricter the demand – that manuscripts should be worked over and over again, until clarity was achieved.

He could not bear . . . our journalese which was so poor, so involved, so dull and incomprehensible. . . . Reading the papers he would be heard exclaiming: 'What language is it written in? Some gibberish! This is double Dutch and not the language of Turgenev or Tolstoy.'

He was also irritated by all the abbreviations which were incomprehensible to the mass of reading workers and peasants. 'You will have to attach a dictionary to every copy of the paper', he used to tell newspaper editors. 'Newspapers are read by the masses and not by individuals who have learnt this new lingo created by our bureaucracy.'[32]

ON MONUMENTAL PROPAGANDA

We have not preserved many of Lenin's indications, direct or indirect, on the role art should play in the creation of socialist culture or on the practical steps which should be taken in this field. This is why I would like to recall his remarkable initiative, dating from the winter of 1918–19. My pleasure in recalling this is all the greater, because we are approaching a time and conditions in which Lenin's ideas can be put into practice in a better way and on a wider scale than they could have been during those years of war, hunger, cold and civil war. I do not remember exactly when it was ... when Lenin asked me to come and see him. I shall allow myself here to reproduce our talk in the form of a dialogue without, of course, guaranteeing the accuracy of each word. ... But I take full responsibility for rendering faithfully the general tone and meaning of the conversation.

'Antony Vassilevich,' started Lenin, 'you certainly have quite a fair number of artists who can produce something and who undoubtedly suffer great hardship.'

'Yes, of course', I said. 'In Moscow and in Petrograd there are more than a few of such men.'

'This concerns sculptors and to a certain extent also poets and writers', went on Lenin. 'For some time I have entertained an idea which I am going to explain to you. You remember that Campanella in his *Civitas Solis* described how the walls of his fantastic socialist city were decorated with frescos which served as a visual lesson in history stirring social conscience – in a word, were part and parcel of the educative and formative endeavour influencing the new generation. This seems to me not at all a naïve idea – with some modifications we could adopt and put it into practice, now.'

I was greatly interested in Lenin's remarks, firstly because they concerned the employment of artists. We had no means to provide them with work and my promises (about how much they stood to gain by changing over from serving the private market to being active within the framework of the State) hung in the air. Apart from this, the use of art for such a worthy aim as educational propaganda of our great idea immediately appealed to me.

Vladimir Ilyich went on: 'Monumental propaganda – this is what I have in mind. First you should get in touch with the Soviet of Moscow and of Petrograd and also organise your artistic resources and then choose appropriate sites. Our climate may not allow us to produce the frescos about which Campanella dreamed. This is why I was talking about sculptors and poets. In many prominent places, on suitable walls or on some special scaffolding there should be scattered short but telling phrases, expressing the essence of the more involved, fundamental Marxist principles and aims, and perhaps also texts giving a condensed version of one or another historical event. Please, do not think that I am imagining marble, granite or gold engraving. For the time being we have to do everything very modestly. Let us have concrete slabs with very clear inscriptions. Just now I am not planning for eternity or even long-term durability of things. Let all this be temporary. Even more important now are monuments with inscriptions: busts, full figures, perhaps bas-reliefs, groups. There should be made a list of the forerunners of socialism, its theoreticians and fighters, and also those torchbearers of philosophical thought, of science, of art, who even without having a direct link with socialism, proved to be real heroes of civilisation.

'According to such a list you should commission artists to do the work, be it even temporary, in plaster, stone or in concrete masonry. Of course, it is important that all this should be accessible to the masses, that propaganda should strike the eye; also that our climate should be remembered: what is produced should not rot, or be destroyed by wind, frost and rain. . . .

'Special attention should be paid to the unveiling of such memorials. We ourselves, our comrades and perhaps prominent scholars should be invited to make a speech. Let every such ceremony become an act of propaganda and a small festivity; then, on the occasion of some anniversary, it might be repeated and people reminded of this or that great man; always, of course, the stress should be laid on the connection with our revolution and our aims.'

To tell you the truth, I was startled and dazzled by these plans, and they appealed to me greatly. Straightway we began implementing them. But the realisation somehow went awry. True, we put up an inscription here and there; also, having attracted a few old and young sculptors, we erected dozens of statues in Leningrad and in Moscow. By no means all the sculptures were successful. If I remember well, Radishchev's and Lassalle's memorials had to be re-made; incidentally, the one to Radishchev can not be found on the same spot where it was originally erected, that is outside the Winter Palace. Maybe some of them survived. I remember a few that were quite good, like Shevchenko's, Herzen's and Chernyshevsky's. Others came out less well, like the one of Marx and Engels, nicknamed by the Muscovites 'Kyril and Methody', as indeed they were made to look like two saints emerging from a bathtub. Our modernists and futurists were particularly wild, and many people became worried at the inhuman representation of Sophie Perovskaya. On the other hand, Bakunin, created by a mature and quite realistic artist Korolev, the author of a very good memorial of Zhelabov . . . was so horrid, that, it was said, even horses bolted at its sight, though in truth not much of Bakunin could be seen from behind a badly constructed fence – the monument was never unveiled.

This was how things went, neither very well, nor very badly. We were more lucky with the unveiling ceremonies. I myself spoke . . . [text unclear as newspaper badly damaged].

It was decided to erect a bust of Marx. The design chosen, after a sizable competition, was that of the sculptor Alyeshin, and it was approved by Lenin. I still regret that this monument was somehow never finished. It was to be placed in the Sverdlov Square. Vladimir Ilyich himself laid the first stone and made a remarkable speech about Marx and about his fiery living spirit which permeated all the stages of the proletarian revolution. . . .[33]

18 September 1918

I heard today Vinogradov's report on the busts and monuments, and am utterly outraged; nothing has been done for months; to this day there is not a single bust; the disappearance of the bust of Radishchev is a farce. There is no bust of Marx on public display, nothing has been done in the way of propaganda by putting up inscriptions in the streets. I reprimand you for this criminal and lackadaisical attitude, and demand that the names of all responsible persons should be sent to me for prosecution. Shame on the saboteurs and thoughtless loafers.

Lenin

Chairman, Council of the
People's Commissars[34]

LENIN ON CINEMA

... About the middle of February, or perhaps towards the end, Vladimir Ilyich proposed that I should come to see him. . . . As far as I remember, we talked about some current problems connected with the Commissariat for Education. Then Lenin asked me what had been done to put into effect his directive of 17 January 1922, set out in the letter to Litkens. I told Lenin in some detail all that I knew about the state of cinematography in the Soviet Republic and about the tremendous difficulties with which it had to contend. I stressed quite especially the Commissariat's lack of means to organise production of films on a large scale and also the lack of specialists in this field, or, to be more precise, lack of communist specialists on whom we could rely. To this Vladimir Ilyich answered that he would try to do something to increase the funds of the cine-photo department, and that he was deeply convinced that this would become a highly profitable business once it was properly set up. He again stressed the necessity to decide on a definite proportion between films providing entertainment and those that were educative. Unfortunately, this remains till this day rather vague. Vladimir Ilyich said that the production of new films, films with communist ideas which would reflect Soviet reality, should start from newsreels and that in his view it might be that the time for making such films had not yet come.

'If you have a good newsreel, serious and illuminating photos, then it is of no importance if in order to attract the public you also show some useless film of a more or less popular type. Of course, censorship is still needed. For counter-revolutionary and immoral films we have no room.'

Then Vladimir Ilyich added:

'Gradually, as we rise to our feet thanks to the correct management of the economy, you may receive, with the improvement in the country's economy, some allowance for this business; you would have to develop film production on a larger scale and offer good quality films to the urban masses and, even more so, to the masses in the countryside.'

Smiling, he said further:

'You are known among us as a patron of art and so you should firmly remember that of all art, the cinema is for us the most important.'

On this, as far as I remember, our talk ended.[35]

V. I. LENIN

DIRECTIVES ON CINEMA

17 January 1922

The People's Commissariat of Education should organise the supervision of all film showings and systematise this enterprise. All films shown in the R.S.F.S.R. [U.S.S.R.] should be registered and numbered at the Commissariat of Education. A definite proportion should be fixed for every film-showing programme:

(a) entertainment films, specially for advertisement or revenue (of course, without obscenity and counter-revolution), and

(b) under the heading 'From the life of peoples of all countries' – pictures with a special propaganda message, such as: Britain's colonial policy in India, the work of the League of Nations, the starving Berliners, etc., etc. Besides films, photographs of propaganda interest should be shown with appropriate subtitles. The privately-owned cinemas should be made to yield a sufficient return to the State in the form of rent, the owners to be allowed to increase the number of films and present new ones subject to censorship by the Commissariat of Education and provided the proper proportion is maintained between entertainment films and propaganda films coming under the heading of films 'From the life of peoples of all countries', in order that film-makers should have an incentive for producing new pictures. They should be allowed wide initiative within these limits. Pictures of a propaganda and educative nature should be checked by old Marxists and writers to avoid a repetition of the many sad instances when our propaganda defeated its own purpose. Special attention should be given to organising performances in the villages and in the east, where films are a novelty and where our propaganda, therefore, will be all the more effective.[36]

A. V. LUNACHARSKY

ON MUSIC   I

Vladimir Ilyich liked music, but it had an unsettling effect on him. There was a time when we had some good concerts in my home. Sometimes Shalyapin would sing; Meychik, Romanovsky, the Stradivarius Quartet or Kussevitzky would play. I often asked Lenin to come, but he was always busy. One day he told me frankly: 'Of course, it's very good to listen to a concert, but, you know, music somehow upsets me – somehow affects me badly!' I remembered that Comrade Tsyurupa, who had succeeded in enticing Lenin to a private performance of the pianist Romanovsky, also told me afterwards that Lenin delighted in his playing, but he was clearly and painfully moved.[37]

ON MUSIC II

It was not true that Lenin did not like music; on the contrary he enjoyed it very much. But, as he himself used to say, music always tired him. . . . 'I am a complete ignoramus in the field of music', he would say; he considered himself an 'ignoramus' because he did not like to listen to any new pieces which he had not known previously – this was what tired him so much. But he delighted in listening to things he had already heard many times before.

I remember how, at his request, I played in his home Beethoven's *Pathétique* and the *Campanella* by Liszt. Ilyich had just returned from a meeting and was exhausted. He said he could not remain seated and asked my permission to pace up and down the room while I was playing. Then he wanted to listen to Schubert-Liszt *Erlkönig*, of which he was very fond.

In 1920, on the occasion of his fiftieth birthday, the Moscow Soviet organised a celebration and a concert. The Shar Trio played Beethoven. Later Ilyich told me and Anna [his sister] that he liked the concert very much, but that it had exhausted him tremendously.

'When I once went to the Opera in Paris,' he used to recall, 'I left feeling utterly tired. Since then I have never gone to the Opera and only very rarely to concerts. . . .'

It was interesting that Vladimir Ilyich who himself had a prodigious memory, was always wondering how people played without music. When I played for him in 1920, he kept on asking how I managed to 'remember it all' and wanted to know whether it was 'terribly difficult' to play from memory.[38]

V WOMEN'S RIGHTS

17 January 1915

†Dear Friend,†

I very much advise you to write the plan of the pamphlet in as much detail as possible.* Otherwise too much is unclear.

One opinion I must express here and now:

I advise you to throw out altogether para. 3 – the '[women's] demand for freedom of love'.

This is not really a proletarian but a bourgeois demand.

After all, what do you understand by that phrase ? What *can* be understood by it ?

1. Freedom *from* material (financial) calculations in affairs of love ?

2. The same, *from* material worries ?

3. From religious prejudices ?

4. From prohibitions by Papa, etc. ?

5. From the prejudices of 'society' ?

6. From the narrow circumstances of one's environment (peasant or petty-bourgeois or bourgeois intellectual) ?

7. From the fetters of the law, the courts and the police ?

8. From the serious element in love ?

9. From child-birth ?

10. Freedom of adultery ? Etc.

I have enumerated many shades (not all, of course). You have in mind, of course, not Nos 8–10 but either Nos 1–7 or something *similar* to Nos 1–7.

But then for Nos 1–7 you must choose a different wording, because freedom of love does not express this idea exactly.

And the public, the readers of the pamphlet, will *inevitably* understand by 'freedom of love', in general, something like Nos 8–10, even *without your wishing it*.

Just because in modern society the most talkative, noisy and 'top' classes understand by 'freedom of love' Nos 8–10, just for that very reason this is not a proletarian but a bourgeois demand.

---

* The pamphlet never appeared in print.

For the proletariat Nos 1-2 are the most important, and then Nos 1-7, and those, in fact, are not 'freedom of love'.

The thing is not what you *subjectively* 'mean' by this. The thing is the *objective logic* of class relations in affairs of love.

†Friendly shake hands!†

W.I.[1]

24 January 1915

Dear Friend,

I apologise for my delay in replying: I wanted to do it yesterday, but was prevented, and I had no time to sit down and write.

As regards your plan for the pamphlet, my opinion was that 'the demand for freedom of love' was unclear and – independently of your will and your wish (I emphasised this when I said that what mattered was the objective class relations, and not your subjective wishes) – would, in present social conditions, turn out to be a bourgeois, not a proletarian, demand.

You do not agree.

Very well. Let us look at the thing again.

In order to make the unclear clear, I enumerated approximately ten *possible* (and, in conditions of class discord, inevitable) different interpretations, and in doing so remarked that interpretations 1-7, in my opinion, would be typical or characteristic of proletarian women, and 8-10 of bourgeois women.

If you are to refute this, you have to show that these interpretations are (1) wrong (and then replace them by others, or indicate which are wrong), or (2) incomplete (then you should add those which are missing), or (3) are not divided into proletarian and bourgeois in that way.

You don't do either one, or the other, or the third.

You don't touch on points 1-7 at all. Does this mean that you admit them to be true (on the whole)? (What you write about the prostitution of proletarian women and their dependence, 'impossibility of saying no', fully comes under points 1-3. No difference at all can be detected between us here.)

Nor do you deny that this is a *proletarian* interpretation.

There remain points 8–10.

These you 'don't quite understand' and 'object' to: 'I do not understand how it is *possible*' (that is what you have written!) 'to *identify*' (!!??) 'freedom of love with point 10. . . .'

So it appears that *I* am 'identifying', while you have undertaken to refute and demolish *me*?

How so?

Bourgeois women understand by freedom of love points 8–10 – that is my thesis.

Do you deny this? Will you say what *bourgeois* ladies understand by freedom of love?

You don't say that. . . .

While you, completely forgetting the objective and class point of view, go over to the 'offensive' against *me*, as though I am 'identifying' freedom of love with points 8–10. . . . Marvellous, really marvellous. . . .

'Even a fleeting passion and intimacy' are 'more poetic and cleaner' than 'kisses without love' of a (vulgar and shallow) married couple. That is what you write. And that is what you intend to write in your pamphlet. Very good.

Is the contrast logical? Kisses without love between a vulgar couple are *dirty*. I agree. To them one should contrast . . . what? . . . One would think: kisses *with* love? While you contrast them with 'fleeting' (why fleeting?) 'passion' (why not love?) – so, logically, it turns out that kisses without love (fleeting) are contrasted with kisses without love by married couple. . . . Strange. For a popular pamphlet would it not be better to contrast philistine-intellectual-peasant . . . vulgar and dirty marriage without love to proletarian, civil marriage with love (adding, *if you absolutely insist*, that fleeting intimacy and passion, too, may be dirty and may be clean). What you have arrived at is not the contrast of class *types*, but something like an 'incident', which of course is possible. But is it a question of particular incidents? If you take the theme of an incident, an individual case of dirty kisses in marriage and pure ones in a fleeting intimacy, that is a theme to be worked out in a novel (because there the whole *essence* is in *individual* circumstances, the analysis of the *characters* and psychology of *particular* types). But in a pamphlet? . . .

Really, I don't want to engage in polemics at all. I would willingly throw aside this letter and postpone matters until we can talk about it. But I want the pamphlet to be a good one, so that *no* one *could* tear out of it phrases which would cause you unpleasantness (sometimes *one single* phrase is enough to be the spoonful of tar in a barrel of honey), *could mis*interpret you[2]. . . .

A GREAT BEGINNING

28 June 1919

... Take the position of women. In this field not a single democratic party in the world, not even in the most advanced bourgeois republic, had done in decades so much as a hundredth part of what we did in our first year in power. We really razed to the ground the infamous laws placing women in a position of inequality, restricting divorce and surrounding it with disgusting formalities, denying recognition to children born out of wedlock, enforcing a search for their fathers, etc. The numerous survivals of these laws, of which the bourgeoisie and capitalism should be ashamed, are to be found in all civilised countries. We have a thousand times the right to be proud of what we have done in this field. But the more *thoroughly* we have cleared the ground of the lumber of the old bourgeois laws and institutions, the more obvious it is to us that we have only cleared the ground to build on but are not yet building.

Notwithstanding all the laws emancipating woman, she continues to be a *domestic slave*, because *petty housework* crushes, strangles, stultifies and degrades her, chains her to the kitchen and the nursery, and she wastes her labour on barbarously unproductive, petty, nerve-racking, stultifying and crushing drudgery. The real *emancipation of women*, real communism, will begin only where and when an all-out struggle begins ... against this petty housekeeping, or rather when its *wholesale transformation* into a large-scale socialist economy begins.

Do we in practice pay sufficient attention to this question, which in theory every communist considers indisputable? Of course not. Do we take proper care of the *shoots* of communism which already exist in this sphere? Again the answer is *no*. Public catering establishments, nurseries, kindergartens – here we have examples of these shoots, here we have the simple, everyday means, involving nothing pompous, grandiloquent or ceremonial, which can *really emancipate women*, really lessen and abolish their inequality with men as regards their role in social production and public life. These means are not new; they (like all the material prerequisites for socialism) were created by large-scale capitalism; but under capitalism they remained, first, a rarity, and secondly – which is particularly important – either *profit-making* enterprises, with all the worst features of speculation, profiteering, cheating and fraud, or 'acrobatics of bourgeois charity', which the best workers rightly hated and despised.[3]

THE TASKS OF THE WORKING WOMEN'S MOVEMENT

23 September 1919

Comrades, it gives me pleasure to greet a conference of working women. I will allow myself to pass over those subjects and questions that, of course, at the moment are the cause of the greatest concern to every working woman and to every politically conscious individual from among the working people: the most urgent questions of bread and war. I know from newspaper reports of your meetings that these have been dealt with exhaustively by Comrade Trotsky as far as they concern the war, and by Comrade Yakovleva and Svidersky as far as they concern the availability of bread. . . .

I should like to say a few words about the general tasks facing the working women's movement in the Soviet Republic, those that are, in general, connected with the transition to socialism, and those that are of particular urgency at the present time. Comrades, the question of the position of women was raised by Soviet power from the very beginning. It seems to me that any workers' state in the course of transition to socialism is faced with a double task. The first part of that task is relatively simple and easy. It concerns those old laws that kept women in a position of inequality as compared to men. . . .

Laws alone, of course, are not enough, and we are by no means content with mere decrees. In the sphere of legislation we have done everything required of us to put women in a position of equality and we have every right to be proud of it. The position of women in Soviet Russia is now ideal as compared with their position in the most advanced States. We tell ourselves, however, that this is only the beginning.

Owing to her work in the house, the woman is still in a difficult position. To effect her complete emancipation and make her the equal of men it is necessary for the national economy to be socialised and for women to participate in common productive labour. Then women will occupy the same position as men.

Here we are not, of course, speaking of making women the equal of men as far as productivity of labour, the quantity of labour, the length of the working day, labour conditions, etc. are concerned; we mean that the woman should not, unlike the man, be oppressed because of her position in the family. You all know that even when women have full rights, they still remain factually downtrodden because all housework is left to them. In most cases, housework is the most unproductive, the most barbarous and the most arduous work a woman can do. It is exceptionally petty and does not in any way promote the development of the woman.

Pursuing the socialist ideal, we want to struggle for the full implementation of socialism, and here an extensive field of labour opens before women. We are now making serious preparations to clear the ground for the building of socialism, but the building of socialism will begin only when we have achieved the complete equality of women and when we undertake the new work together with women who have been emancipated from that petty, stultifying, unproductive work. This is a job that will take us many many years. . . .

We say that the emancipation of the workers must be effected by the workers themselves, and in exactly the same way the emancipation of working women is a matter for the working women themselves. The working women must themselves see to it that such institutions [which will emancipate women from housework – dining-rooms, nurseries, etc.] are developed, and this activity will bring about a complete change in their position from what it was in the old, capitalist society. . . .[4]

SOVIET POWER AND THE STATUS OF WOMEN

6 November 1919

The second anniversary of Soviet power is an occasion for taking stock of what has been done during this period and for reflecting on the significance and the aims of the revolution that has been accomplished.

The bourgeoisie and its supporters charge us with having violated democracy. We, on the other hand, assert that the Soviet revolution has given an unprecedented impulse to the development of democracy in breadth and depth, democracy, that is, for the working people oppressed by capitalism; democracy for the overwhelming majority of the people, socialist democracy (for the working people), as distinct from bourgeois democracy (for the exploiters, for the capitalists, for the rich).

Who is right?

To give proper thought to this question and to achieve a deeper understanding of it one must take stock of the experience of these two years and make better preparations for further development.

The status of women makes clear in the most striking fashion the difference between bourgeois and socialist democracy and furnishes a most effective reply to the question posed.

In a bourgeois republic (that is, where there is private ownership of land, factories, shares, etc.), be it the most democratic republic, women have never had rights fully equal to those of men *anywhere in the world, in any one of the more advanced countries*. And this despite the fact that more than 125 years have passed since the great French (bourgeois-democratic) revolution.

In words, bourgeois democracy promises equality and freedom, but in practice *not a single* bourgeois republic, even the most advanced, has granted women (half the human race) complete equality with men in the eyes of the law, or delivered women from dependence on and oppression by the male.

Bourgeois democracy is the democracy of pompous phrases, solemn words, lavish promises and high-sounding slogans about *freedom and equality*, but in practice all this cloaks the lack of freedom and equality for the working and exploited people.

Soviet or socialist democracy sweeps away these pompous but false words and declares ruthless war on the hypocrisy of 'democrats', landowners, capitalists and farmers with bursting bins who are piling up wealth by selling surplus grain to the starving workers at profiteering prices.

Down with this foul lie! There is no 'equality', nor can there be, of oppressed and oppressor, exploited and exploiter. There is no real 'freedom', nor can there be, so long as women are handicapped by men's legal privileges, so long as there is no freedom for the worker from the yoke of capital, no freedom for the labouring peasant from the yoke of the capitalist, landowner and merchant.

Let the liars and the hypocrites, the obtuse and the blind, the bourgeois and their supporters, try to deceive the people with talk about freedom in general, about equality in general, and about democracy in general.

We say to the workers and peasants – tear the mask from these liars, open the eyes of the blind. Ask them:

> Is there equality of the two sexes?
> Which nation is the equal of which?
> *Which class is the equal of which?*

Freedom from what yoke or from the yoke of which class? Freedom for which class? He who speaks about politics, democracy and freedom, about equality, about socialism *without posing* these questions, without giving them priority, who does not fight against hushing them up, concealing and blunting them, is the worst enemy of the working people, a wolf in sheep's clothing, the rabid opponent of the workers and peasants, a lackey of the landowners, the tsars and the capitalists.

In the course of two years of Soviet power in one of the most backward countries of Europe more has been done to emancipate woman, to make her the equal of the 'strong' sex than has been done during the past 130 years by all advanced, enlightened, 'democratic' republics of the world taken together. . . .[5]

ON LOVE IN COMMUNIST SOCIETY

It was in Lenin's large study in the Kremlin in the autumn of 1920 that we had our first long conversation on the subject [of women's communist movement].

'We must create a powerful international women's movement, on a clear theoretical basis', Lenin began after having greeted me. 'There is no good practice without Marxist theory, that is clear. The greatest clarity of principle is necessary for us communists on this question. . . .

'The energy, willingness and enthusiasm of women comrades, their courage and wisdom in times of illegality or semi-legality indicate good prospects for the development of our work. . . . What makes your comrades, the proletarian women of Germany, enthusiastic? What about their proletarian class consciousness; are their interests, their activities concentrated on immediate political demands? What is the mainspring of their ideas?

'I have heard some peculiar things on this matter from Russian and German comrades, I must tell you. I was told that a talented woman communist in Hamburg is publishing a paper for prostitutes and that she wants to organise them for the revolutionary fight. Rosa [Luxemburg] acted and felt as a Communist when in an article she championed the cause of the prostitutes who were imprisoned for any transgression of police regulations in carrying on their dreary trade. They are, unfortunately, doubly sacrificed by bourgeois society. First by its accursed property system, and secondly by its accursed moral hypocrisy. That is obvious. Only he who is brutal or shortsighted can forget it. But still, that is not at all the same thing as considering prostitutes – how shall I put it? – to be a special revolutionary militant section, as organising them and publishing a factory paper for them. Aren't there really any other working women in Germany to organise, for whom a paper can be issued, who must be drawn into your struggles? The other is only a diseased excrescence. It reminds me of the literary fashion of painting every prostitute as a sweet Madonna. The origin of that was healthy too: social sympathy, rebellion against the virtuous hypocrisy of the respectable bourgeois. But the healthy part became corrupted and degenerate. Besides, the question of prostitutes will give rise to many serious problems here. Take them back to productive work, bring them into the social economy. That is what we must do. . . .

'I was told that questions of sex and marriage are the main subjects dealt with in the reading and discussion evenings of women comrades. They are the chief subject of interest, of political instruction and education. I could scarcely believe my ears when I heard this. . . . The situation in Germany itself requires the greatest possible concentration of all proletarian revolutionary forces to defeat the ever-growing and ever-increasing counter-revolution. But working women comrades discuss sexual problems and the question of forms of marriage in the past, present and future. They think it their most important duty to enlighten proletarian women on these subjects. . . .

'It seems to me that these flourishing sexual theories which are mainly hypothetical, and often quite arbitrary, arise from the personal need to justify personal abnormality or hypertrophy in sexual life before bourgeois morality, and to entreat its patience. This masked respect for bourgeois morality seems to me just as repulsive as interfering in sexual matters. However wild and revolutionary the behaviour may be, it is still really quite bourgeois. It is, mainly, a hobby of the intellectuals and of the sections nearest to them. There is no place for it in the party, in the class conscious, fighting proletariat.

'. . . And what is the result of this futile, un-Marxist way of dealing with all this? That the great social question appears as an adjunct, as a part, of sexual problems. The main thing becomes a subsidiary matter. That does not only endanger clarity on that question itself, it muddles the thoughts, the class consciousness of proletarian women generally. . . . Is now the time to amuse proletarian women with discussions on how one loves and is loved, how one marries and is married? . . .

'The youth movement too is attacked by the disease of modernity in its attitude towards sexual questions and in being exaggeratedly concerned with them. . . . I have been told that sexual questions are the favourite study of your youth organisations, too. There is supposed to be a lack of speakers on this subject. Such misconceptions are particularly harmful, particularly dangerous in the youth movement. . . . Sex and marriage forms, in their bourgeois sense, are unsatisfactory. A revolution in sex and marriage is approaching, corresponding to the proletarian revolution. It is easily comprehensible that these very involved problems. . . should occupy the mind of youth, as well as of women. They suffer particularly under present-day sexual grievances. They are rebelling with all the impetuosity of their years. We can understand that. Nothing could be more false than to preach the asceticism of monks and the sanctity of dirty bourgeois morality to the youth. . . . Although I am anything but a gloomy ascetic, the so-called "new sexual life" often seems to me to be purely bourgeois, an extension of bourgeois brothels, but has nothing whatever in common with freedom of love as we communists understand it. You must be aware of the famous theory that in communist society the satisfaction of sexual desires, of love, will be as simple and unimportant as drinking a glass of water. This glass-of-water theory has made our young people mad, quite mad. It has proved fatal to many young boys and girls. Its adherents maintain that it is Marxist . . . [while] it is completely un-Marxist, and moreover, antisocial. In sexual life there is not only simple nature to be considered, but also cultural characteristics, whether they are of a high or low order. . . . Of course, thirst must be satisfied. But would normal man in normal circumstances lie down in the gutter and drink out of a puddle, or out of a glass with a rim greasy from many lips ? But the social aspect is most important of all. The drinking of water is of course an individual affair. But in love two lives are concerned, and a third, a new life, arises. It is that which gives it its social interest, which gives rise to a duty towards the community.

'As a communist I have not the least sympathy for the glass of water theory, although it bears the fine title "satisfaction of love". In any case, this liberation of love is neither new, nor communistic. You will remember that about the middle of the last century it was preached as the "emancipation of the heart" in romantic literature. In bourgeois practice it became the emancipation of the flesh. At that time the preaching was more talented than it is today, and as for the practice, I cannot judge. I do not mean to preach asceticism by my criticism. Not in the least. Communism will not bring asceticism, but joy of life, power of life, and a satisfied love life will help to do that. . . .

'The revolution demands concentration, increase of forces. From masses, from individuals. It cannot tolerate orgiastic conditions, such as are normal for the decadent heroes and heroines of D'Annunzio. Dissoluteness in sexual life is bourgeois, is a phenomenon of decay. The proletariat is a rising class. It does not need intoxication as a narcotic or a stimulus. Intoxication as little by sexual exaggeration as by alcohol. It must not and shall not forget the shame, the filth, the savagery of capitalism. It receives the strongest urge to fight from a class situation, from the communist ideal. It needs clarity, clarity, and again clarity. And so I repeat, no weakening, no destruction of forces. Self-control, self-discipline is not slavery, not even in love. . . .

'The inseparable connection between the social and human position of the woman and private property in the means of production must be strongly brought out. That will draw a clear and ineradicable line of distinction between our policy and feminism. And it will also supply the basis for regarding the woman question as a part of the social question, of the workers' problem, and so bind it firmly to the proletarian class struggle and the revolution. . . . Our ideological conceptions dictate the principles of organisation: no special organisations for women. A woman communist is a member of the party just as a man communist.'[6]

VI BUREAUCRACY

LENIN AND THE PEASANTS

A flood of letters, complaints, pleas and requests from all over the country began to pour in at the office of the Chairman of the People's Commissars soon after it was properly organised. There were also numerous delegations, deputations, and go-betweens coming mostly from the countryside. It was my duty to receive most of these visitors. Their problems were indeed manifold. The government was only just beginning to take shape in the countryside, among the peasants. Everywhere there were gangs roaming the provinces, trying to live at somebody else's expense, and pretending to act in the name of some revolutionary organisation; they were engaged in terrorism, plunder, robbery, drunkenness and all manner of other depredations. Local people suffered all this without knowing to whom to turn for help and how to defend themselves. . . .

Vladimir Ilyich wished to have some personal contact with the peasants. He set apart a special day – Friday – for the meetings. . . . This was at the beginning of 1919. . . . His first meeting with the peasants took place in his Kremlin office. We assembled the delegates in the waiting-room and only ten minutes before the meeting we told them that they would have a talk with the Chairman of the People's Commissars himself. At the prospect of seeing Vladimir Ilyich the peasants became enthusiastic. Their voices grew livelier and they acquired new courage. They moved towards Vladimir Ilyich's office, leaving in the waiting-room their bags, sacks and bundles with which they usually travelled. The sentry at the door . . . let them pass. And so the delegates from Penza, and Kursk, Smolensk and Samara . . . decorously, without haste, entered the room of the Chairman of the People's Commissars.

There was a moment of solemn silence. Vladimir Ilyich got up and looked at them.

Then a chorus of voices:

'Good-day, Vladimir Ilyich' – and all bowed deeply.

'Good-day, good-day', Vladimir Ilyich greeted them,

moving from behind his table and shaking hands with everyone. 'Please, sit down, please, here. And you, grandfather, sit on the sofa, that's it.'

He himself sat on a stool beside the table so as to be able to see them all, and asked kindly:

'Well, what brought you here?'

'We have a great deal of business.'

'A tremendous amount!'

'Well, about the land!'

'We are being insulted!'

'You judge. . . .'

'If you are the governor, you should know all. . . .'*

And the 'voices of the soil' were raised and were heard. One or two unbuttoned their tunics and reached into their pockets for the 'document', the written 'petition' where everything was set out. For a 'clever man' it was enough to read these papers, immediately to understand and to resolve all the most distressing problems.

When it became somewhat quieter, Vladimir Ilyich asked each one from what district, what village he came, and – what always amazed me – he at once remembered the answers. Later on, during the conversation, he addressed each person mentioning his place of origin. The peasants, too, noted this and were greatly surprised. . . .

'And what did you come about?' Vladimir Ilyich asked a big black-haired peasant from the Penza District.

'Well, it is about the government.'

'What in particular?'

'We had elections. . . .'

'Well. . . .'

'And so we elected our citizens to the Soviet. And when they went into the Soviet, they took up arms, they armed themselves and began to oppress us, and opp – ppress us. . . now there is no life. . . . Free us from them. . . .'

'How do they oppress you, in what way. . . ?'

'They oppress us from morning till night, there is nowhere to escape to. It's terrible, nowhere to run away to, I even came

---

* The peasants addressed Lenin in the second person singular – thou.

to you in secret because if they knew they would arrest me and throw me into jail – to feed the lice.'

'What do they actually do?'

'Everything! They take our things away, they make us pay fines . . . took bread and flour to register for storing but carried it all off for themselves. . . .'

'How can that be?' exclaimed Vladimir Ilyich. 'These are your people, chosen by yourselves, so they must be good, just people. . . .'

'Yes, that's how it is, they are our people, but in truth. . . . And as for justice – there is no justice. . . .'

'Why?'

'Well, they are all big horse-thieves, swindlers, how shall I put it, simply jail-birds – they were jail-birds and remain jail-birds. . . .' burst out the Penza giant, getting up nervously.

'How did that happen? But you yourselves have elected them.'

'Yes, it's true, we elected them. . . .'

'Then why did you act so rashly?'

The big man stood silent, then rubbed his cap, shook his tussled hair, looked around and said:

'We elected them because they were used to being locked up in jails . . . .'

A sympathetic murmur went around.

'Why in jail? Why should representatives of the Soviet administration be locked up in jails?' asked Vladimir Ilyich, greatly puzzled.

'Well, to tell you the whole truth: we did not believe that we would have our own government; we thought it wouldn't last long, that some kind of troops would come along and disperse it all, and as to the officials – these would be the first to be caught and shoved into prison. . . . And so, well, the jail-birds – they are used, these horse-thieves, to being locked up and so they would not mind so much, while us – we are farmers and we are not fit for that. . . . And instead, they got hold of power and began to oppress us, oppress us, oppress us. . . .'

Vladimir Ilyich laughed heartily; it was quite impossible to refrain from laughing at this tragicomic tale.

'You see, you made a mistake. Soviet power is truly people's power at the head of which stands the working class', said Lenin. 'Now you see that you should have elected the best, the most honest, the most conscientious people. You see where you have landed yourselves by not trusting your own government which finally put an end to the power of the tsar, the landlords, the traders, the rich, and the possessing classes.'

'Yes, we see that we made a mistake. . . .'

'And how long is it since you elected these, your officials that oppress you?'

'Nearly three months ago.'

'As you know, delegates to the Soviet are elected every six months. Only then can you remove all the bad ones and replace them by others, making sure that your own administration is really good.'

'Yes, that's right and proper', answered the man from Penza. One heard approving noises from the other delegates. . . .

At this first meeting Lenin spent nearly five hours listening to all the complaints and dealing with them in an appropriate manner. . . .

A few days later a special office was opened in town because it became clear that many people from the provinces could not find their way into the Kremlin as they were unable to explain what they wanted; the commandant of the guards was overburdened with the task of checking the identity of the multitude of applicants who had been told to get in touch with members of the government. He was only too glad to see the office for peasants' complaints removed from the Kremlin.

. . . A reception centre was organised near the Kremlin, in Mokhova Street. Apart from the waiting-room there were large rooms where the delegates could sit down, have a rest and even take some tea and where they could also write down their demands. Those who could not write were helped by employees of the administrative offices of the Presidium of the People's Commissars. For this work I enlisted also the services of a few thoughtful and responsible workers and Red Army men. . . .

On the first day I was receiving people for eight solid hours with hardly any break. Everybody was questioned about his difficulties and needs, the replies were noted in a book, and his problems were dealt with. On the spot I wrote in great detail to whom the applicant should address himself and what he should do. There was a strict rule that our office was to follow up all the affairs of people who in the first instance came to us, but who, in order to get full satisfaction, had to be sent to some other commissariat. I must say straightway that the persistence with which we watched over all our applicants was not at all to the taste of some other authorities. Vladimir Ilyich was often told that the Administrative Office of the Sovnarkom was flooding other commissariats with all manner of problems and affairs.

Vladimir Ilyich used to laugh outright at this kind of grumbling, saying:

'Look at that, we have hardly made the revolution and chased away one set of officials from their well-worn seats, and already our own officials got bureaucratised to such a degree that they are displeased when the people rightly concerned with their own needs, present them with petitions and complaints. You tell me, which of our laws says that any citizen of our country is not entitled to complain, to demand or to fight for what is due to him from a given authority? It is strange and absolutely shameful to hear such statements. We have set up our governmental apparatus precisely for this purpose: that after the defeat of the bourgeoisie and the ruling classes, it should facilitate life for those who previously had been exploited. When it comes to the test, it turns out that we ourselves have not yet shaken off [the old methods]. . . . This is no good. It has to be fought against with all our strength.'

And Vladimir Ilyich insisted that a Complaints' Office should be organised, which would deal with the grievances of the whole population against all possible irregularities and particularly with complaints against our own administration.'[1]

V. I. LENIN

THE PARTY CRISIS

19 January 1921

. . . While dealing with the discussion which took place on 30 December, I must correct another mistake of mine. I said: 'Ours is not actually a workers' State but a workers' and peasants' State.' Comrade Bukharin immediately exclaimed: 'What kind of State?' In reply I referred him to the Eighth Congress of Soviets, which had just closed. I went back to the report of that discussion and found that I was wrong and Comrade Bukharin was right. What I should have said is: 'A workers' State is an abstraction. What we actually have is a workers' State, with this peculiarity, firstly, that it is not the working class but the peasant population that predominates in the country, and secondly, that it is a workers' State with bureaucratic distortions. . . .'[2]

V. I. LENIN

INTERNATIONAL AND DOMESTIC SITUATION

6 March 1922

... We have given communists, with all their splendid qualities, practical executive jobs for which they are totally unfitted. How many communists are there in government offices? We have huge quantities of material, bulky works, that would cause the heart of the most methodical German scientist to rejoice; we have mountains of paper, and it would take *Istpart** fifty times fifty years to go through it all; but if you tried to find anything practical in a State trust, you would fail; and you would never know who was responsible for what. The practical fulfilment of decrees – of which we had more than enough, and which we manufacture as fast as Mayakovsky described – is never checked. Are the orders of the responsible communist officials carried out? Can they get this done? No. They cannot; and that is why we are changing our domestic policy to the core. Of what value are our meetings and commissions? Very often they are just make-believe. ...

... Our worst internal enemy is the bureaucrat – the communist who occupies a responsible (or not responsible) Soviet post and enjoys universal respect as a conscientious man. As the Russian saying goes: 'Although he never touches a drop, he sings false.' He is very conscientious, but he has not learnt to combat red tape, he is unable to combat it, he condones it. We must rid ourselves of this enemy, and with the aid of all class-conscious workers and peasants we shall get at him. The whole mass of the non-party workers and peasants will follow the lead of the vanguard of the communist party in the fight against this enemy and this inefficiency and Oblomovism. There must be no hesitation whatever in this matter. ...[3]

---

* Commission for collecting and studying material on the history of the revolution and the history of the party.

CONDITIONS FOR ADMITTING NEW MEMBERS TO THE PARTY

26 March 1922

... There is no doubt that judged by the bulk of its present membership, our party is not proletarian enough. I do not thing anybody can challenge this, and a mere glance at the statistics will bear it out. Since the war, the industrial workers of Russia have become much less proletarian than they were before, because during the war all those who desired to evade military service went into the factories. This is common knowledge. On the other hand it is equally undoubted that taken as a whole (if we take the level of the overwhelming majority of party members), our party is less politically trained than is necessary for real proletarian leadership in the present difficult situation, especially in view of the tremendous preponderance of the peasantry rapidly awakening to independent class politics. Further, it must be borne in mind that the temptation to join the ruling party at the present time is very great. It is sufficient to recall all the literary productions of the *Smena Vekh* writers to see that the types who have been carried away by the political successes of the Bolsheviks are very remote from everything proletarian. If the Genoa Conference* results in further political successes for us, there will be a big increase in the efforts of petty-bourgeois elements, and of elements positively hostile to all that is proletarian, to penetrate into the party. Six months' probation for workers will not diminish this pressure in the least, because it is the easiest thing in the world for anyone to qualify for this short probation period by fraudulent means, the more so as it is not at all difficult under present conditions for many intellectual and semi-intellectual elements to join the ranks of the workers. From all this I draw the conclusion that we must establish much longer probation periods and this opinion is strengthened by the fact that the

* The International Economic and Financial Conference of April-May 1922 held on the initiative of the Soviet government; representatives of twenty-nine countries attended.

white-guards are definitely banking on the non-proletarian composition of our party membership. If we agree to a six months' period for workers, we must without fail, in order not to deceive ourselves and others, define the term 'worker' in such a way as to include only those who have acquired a proletarian mentality from their very conditions of life. But this is impossible unless the persons concerned have worked in a factory for many years – not from ulterior motives, but because of the general conditions of their economic and social life.

If we do not close our eyes to reality we must admit that at the present time the proletarian policy of the party is not determined by the character of its membership, but by the enormous undivided prestige enjoyed by the small group which might be called the Old Guard of the party. A slight conflict within this group will be enough, if not to destroy this prestige, at all events to weaken the group to such a degree as to rob it of its power to determine policy.[4]

ELEVENTH CONGRESS OF THE R.C.P.(b)

27 March 1922

... The vehicle is pulling out of hand: it is as if there were someone driving it and the car were going not in the direction in which he steers it, but in the direction someone else is steering it; as if the car were driven by some illegal, lawless hand; god knows whose, perhaps by a speculator's, perhaps by a private capitalist's or perhaps by both. Be that as it may, the vehicle is not going quite in the direction the man at the wheel imagines, and very often it goes in quite a different direction. . . . [5]

... Wherein lies our strength and what do we lack? We have quite enough political power. I hardly think there is anyone here who will assert that on such-and-such a practical question, in such-and-such a business institution, the communists, the communist party, lack sufficient power. There are people who think only of this, but these people are hopelessly looking backwards and cannot understand that one must look ahead. The main economic power is in our hands. All the vital large enterprises, the railways, etc., are in our hands. The number of leased enterprises, although considerable in places, is on the whole insignificant; altogether it is infinitesimal compared with the rest. The economic power in the hands of the proletarian State of Russia is quite adequate to ensure the transition to communism. What then is lacking? Obviously, what is lacking is culture among the stratum of the communists who perform administrative functions. If we take Moscow with its 4,700 communists in responsible positions, and if we take that huge bureaucratic machine, that gigantic heap, we must ask: who is directing whom? I doubt very much whether it can truthfully be said that the communists are directing that heap. To tell the truth, they are not directing, they are being directed. Something analogous happened here to what we were told in our history lessons when we were children: sometimes one nation conquers another, the nation that conquers is victorious and

the nation that is conquered is defeated. This is simple and intelligible to all. But what happens to the culture of these nations?
Here things are not so simple. If the conquering nation has a
higher level of culture than the vanquished nation, the former
imposes its culture upon the latter; but if the opposite is the case,
the vanquished nation imposes its culture upon its conqueror.
Has not something like this happened in the capital of the
R.S.F.S.R.? Have the 4,700 communists (nearly a whole army division, and all of them the very best) come under the influence of
an alien culture? True, there may be the impression that the
vanquished have a high level of culture. But that is not the case
at all. Their culture is miserable, insignificant, but it is still at a
higher level than ours. Miserable and low as it is, it is higher than
that of our responsible communist administrators, for the latter
lack administrative ability. Communists who are put at the head
of departments – and sometimes artful saboteurs deliberately put
them in these positions in order to use them as a shield – are
often fooled. This is a very unpleasant admission to make, or,
at any rate, not a very pleasant one; but I think we must admit
it, for at present this is the salient problem. I think that this is
the political lesson of the past year; and it is around this that the
struggle will rage in 1922.

Will the responsible communists of the R.S.F.S.R. and of the
Russian communist party realise that they cannot administer;
that they only imagine they are directing, but are, actually,
being directed? If they realise this they will learn, of course, for
this can be learnt. But one must study hard to learn it, and our
people are not doing this. They scatter orders and decrees right
and left, but the result is quite different from what they want. . . .

The idea of building communist society exclusively with
the hands of the communists is childish, absolutely childish. We
communists are but a drop in the ocean, a drop in the ocean of
the people. . . .

In the sea of people we are after all but a drop in the ocean,
and we can administer only when we express correctly what the
people are conscious of. Unless we do this, the communist
party will not lead the proletariat, the proletariat will not lead
the masses, and the whole machine will collapse. The chief
thing that the people, all the working people, want today is

practical help in their desperate poverty and hunger; they want to see that the improvement needed by the peasants is really taking place in the form to which they are accustomed. The peasant knows and is accustomed to the market and trade. We were unable to introduce direct communist distribution. We lacked the factories and their equipment for this. And so we have to provide the peasants with what they need through trade, and provide it as well as the capitalists did, otherwise people will not tolerate such an administration. This is the key to the situation. And unless something unexpected arises, this ... should be the central feature of our activities in 1922. ...

In conclusion I must mention the practical side of the question of our Soviet institutions, the higher government bodies and the party's relation to them. The relations between the party and the Soviet government bodies are not what they ought to be; on this we all absolutely agree. I have given one example of how minor matters are dragged before the Political Bureau. It is extremely difficult to get out of this by formal means, for there is only one ruling party in our country; and a member of the party cannot be prohibited from lodging complaints. That is why everything that is brought before the Council of the People's Commissars and the Political Bureau went through my hands. When I was obliged to retire from work, it was found that the two wheels were not working in unison and Kamenev had to bear a treble load to maintain this contact. In as much as it is hardly probable that I shall return to work in the near future, all hope devolves on the fact that there are two other deputies. . . . . .[6]

NOTE TO L. B. KAMENEV ON THE STRUGGLE AGAINST GREAT RUSSIAN CHAUVINISM

6 October 1922

Comrade Kamenev! I declare war to the death on Great Russian chauvinism. As soon as I get rid of this accursed aching tooth, I shall bite into it with all my healthy teeth.

It must be *absolutely* insisted that the Union Central Executive Committee should be *presided over* in turn by a

Russian,
Ukranian,
Georgian, and so forth.
Absolutely!

Yours,

Lenin[7]

TO THE PRESIDIUM OF THE FIFTH CONGRESS OF THE SOVIET EMPLOYEES' UNION

22 November 1922

Dear Comrades,

The primary, immediate task of the present day, and of the next few years, is systematically to reduce the size and the cost of the Soviet machinery of State by cutting down staffs, improving organisation, eliminating red tape and bureaucracy, and by reducing unproductive expenditure. In this field your Union has a great deal of work before it.

Wishing the Fifth All Russian Congress of the Soviet Employees' Union success and fruitful work, I hope that it will especially deal with the question of the Soviet machinery of State.

V. Ulyanov (Lenin)

Chairman of the Council of the People's Commissars[8]

LENIN'S LAST NOTES: ON THE QUESTION OF NATIONALITIES OR ON 'AUTONOMISATION'

Dictated on 30–1 December 1922

I am, it seems, strongly guilty before the workers of Russia for not having intervened vigorously and drastically enough in this notorious issue of autonomisation, officially called, I think, the question of the union of the Soviet Socialist Republics.

In summer, when this issue came to the fore, I was ill; later on, in the autumn, I entertained exaggerated hopes as to my recovery and I expected that the October and December plenum would give me a possibility to intervene in this matter. But, in the meantime, neither in the October plenary meeting (on the subject) nor in the December one could I be present and so the problem nearly completely passed me by.

I had just time for a talk with Comrade Dzerzhinsky who came from the Caucasus and told me about the situation in Georgia. I also managed to exchange a few words with Comrade Zinoviev and express to him my fears as regards this question. What I was told by Comrade Dzerzhinsky, who headed the commission sent by the Central Committee to 'investigate' the Georgian incident, could only arouse my greatest fears. If things went so far that Ordjonikidze could rush and resort to the use of physical force, as Comrade Dzerzhinsky told me, then one can imagine into what a swamp we have descended. Obviously, the whole device of 'autonomisation' was essentially wrong and untimely.

It was said that there was need for a unified apparatus. Where did such ideas emanate from? Did they not come from the same apparatus . . . which [we had] borrowed from tsardom and only just covered with a Soviet veneer?

Undoubtedly, we should have waited with this measure until we were able to say that we take responsibility for this apparatus as if it were our own. Now we have in all conscience to say the opposite, that we are calling ours the apparatus which in fact is still through and through alien to us and represents a bourgeois and tsarist mixture which we had no possibility whatsoever to remake in five years without help from other countries, and at the time when military 'preoccupations' and the struggle against hunger predominated.

In such circumstances it is quite natural that 'the freedom of secession from the Union' by which we justify ourselves, will prove nothing more but a scrap of paper which would not protect the Russian nationalites from the irruption of that truly Russian man, the Great Russian chauvinist who is essentially a scoundrel and an oppressor as is the typical Russian bureaucrat. There is no doubt that the insignificant percentage of the Soviet and sovietised workers will drown in this sea of the chauvinist Great Russian mob, like a fly in milk.

I think that . . . Stalin's rashness and administrative zeal played a fatal role as also did his spite against the famous 'social-nationalism'. In politics, spite plays generally the worst possible role.

I am also afraid that Comrade Dzerzhinsky, who travelled to the Caucasus to investigate the 'offences' of those 'social-nationals', has distinguished himself by his truly Russian state of mind (it is well-known that Russified aliens are always much more Russian than the Russians themselves)* and that the impartiality of his whole commission was sufficiently characterised by Ordjonikidze's 'use of the fist'. To my mind this Russian use of the fist cannot be justified by any provocation nor by any affront, and that Comrade Dzerzhinsky is irreparably guilty of adopting a lightminded attitude towards that 'use of the fist'.

Ordjonikidze was the authority as far as all the other citizens of the Caucasus were concerned. Ordjonikidze had no right to that irritation which he and Dzerzhinsky mentioned. On the contrary, Ordjonikidze's duty was to behave with a restraint not demanded of any ordinary citizen, and still less of one who is accused of a 'political' offence. . . .

---

* Dzerzhinsky was of Polish origin.

In my previous writings I have already said that there is no use posing the problem of nationalism in the abstract. It is necessary to distinguish between the nationalism of the oppressing nation and that of the oppressed, the nationalism of a big nation and that of a small one.

Nearly always in history the practice was that we, members of a big nation, have proved guilty of an unending number of oppressive acts, and what is more – without noticing it ourselves – we commit oppressive deeds and offences; it is enough to recall my Volga reminiscences about how the minorities are treated, how a Pole is never called anything else but 'Polyachishka', a Tartar is mocked by the name of 'Knyaz' (prince), and a Ukrainian 'Khokhol', while the Georgians and other Caucasians are referred to as 'the Capcasus men'.

This is why internationalism on the part of a . . . so-called great nation (great only through its acts of oppression, great only in the sense in which the bully may claim to be great) should consist not merely in respecting formal equality between nations. It is necessary to create such equality that would reduce . . . the actual inequality which arises in practical life. Who has not understood this has not understood the truly proletarian attitude towards the problem of nationalities. . . .

It is not only important but it is absolutely essential to give the proletariat of the small nation real confidence in the proletarian struggle [of the big nation]. . . . For this not only formal equality is needed. For this one has to compensate – in one way or another, by one's behaviour or one's concessions – for the lack of confidence, for the suspiciousness, the offences, which in the past the members of the small nation suffered from the rulers of the 'great' power.

It seems that for Bolsheviks, for communists, further detailed explanations are not needed . . . nothing hampers the growth and consolidation of proletarian class solidarity as much as does injustice towards smaller nationalites. . . . That is why . . . it is better to show towards national minorities too much conciliation and softness, rather than too little. . . .[9]

GLOSSARY

Abramovich, R. (1880–1963): one of the leaders of the *Bund*; a prominent Menshevik.

Alexinsky, G. A. (b. 1879): left the bolsheviks after the defeat of the 1905 revolution; after 1918 an anti-bolshevik emigré.

Arakcheev, A. A. (1769–1834): one of the most reactionary of Alexander I's Ministers; his name is synonymous with a brutal military regime.

Bagotsky, S. J. (1879–1953): as secretary of the Committee of Aid to Political Prisoners, was asked in 1912 to render all possible assistance to Lenin and his wife.

Bakunin, M. A. (1814–1876): the founder of anarchism.

Balabanoff, A. (1876–1965): an Italian socialist of Russian origin; excellent linguist; acted as the secretary at the founding Congress of the Communist International.

Bernstein, E. (1850–1932): the leader of revisionist Marxism; theoretician of reformism and Social-Democracy.

Biron, E. I. (1690–1772): a corrupt court favourite of Empress Anne; the regent after her death.

Blanqui, L.- A. (1805–1881): a prominent representative of French utopian communism.

Bobrovskaya (Zelikson) Ts. S. (1876–1960): party activist since 1898; represented *Iskra* in the south of Russia; between 1928 and 1940 an employee of the Communist International.

Bonch-Bruevich, V. D. (1873–1955): active revolutionary since the 1880s; from 1917 to 1920 responsible for the administration of the Council of the People's Commissars; historian, ethnographer and author.

Bukharin, N. I. (1888–1938): member of the Bolshevik Old Guard; perished in Stalin's Purges.

Bund: popular name for the All-Jewish Workers' League, part of the Social-Democratic movement; the *Bund* became strongly pro-Menshevik.

Cadets: liberal party Constitutional Democrats, favouring constitutional monarchy.

Campanella, T. (1558–1639): Italian Renaissance philosopher.

Cheka: Extraordinary Commission to Fight Counter-Revolution and Espionage; later G.P.U., State Security.

Chicherin, G. V. (1872–1936): an old Bolshevik; from 1918 to 1930 Commissar for Foreign Affairs.

Comsomol: Young Communist League.

Decembrists: revolutionary noblemen of 1825.

Denikin, A. I. (1872–1947): one of the commanders in chief of the White Guard during the civil war.

Dobrolyubov, N. A. (1836–1861): Russian revolutionary writer, literary critic and poet.

Dzerzhinsky, F. E. (1877–1926): head of the *Cheka.*

Economism: a trend among Russian Social-Democrats, which laid emphasis on trade-union activities rather than on political struggle.

Emancipation of the serfs: see footnote, p. 140.

Essen, M. M. (1872–1956): began her revolutionary career in the 1890s; after 1920 active in Georgia; worked later on in the Lenin Institute concerned with party history.

February 1917 revolution: led to the abolition of the monarchy.

Gil, S.K. (b. 1888): Lenin's chauffeur and bodyguard from 1917 to 1924.

Goncharov, I. A. (1812–1891): Russian novelist; worked for a time as an official censor.

Gorky, A. M. (1868–1936): a prominent Russian-Soviet writer.

Humbert-Droz, J. (1891–1971): Swiss pacifist; later a communist and an official of the Communist International.

Huysmans, C. (1871–1968): leader of the Belgian labour movement; Secretary of the International Bureau of the Second International.

Kalinin, M. I. (1875–1946): member of the Bolshevik Old Guard; regarded as the spokesman of the peasants; President of the Supreme Council of the U.S.S.R.

Kamenev, L. B. (1883–1936): prominent member of the bolshevik Old Guard; perished in Stalin's Purges.

Kautsky, K. (1854–1938): one of the foremost theoreticians of Marxism; later a reformist.

Kerensky, A. F. (1881–1970): after February 1917 Minister of Justice and of war; Prime Minister of the Provisional government until the October revolution.

Kolchak, A. L. (1873–1920): admiral; one of the chief commanders of the counter-revolution.

Kollontay, A. M. (1872–1952): Russian revolutionary; bolshevik; member of the Workers' Opposition; in the diplomatic service from 1923.

Kolokol (The Bell): published by Herzen between 1857 and 1869; the most influential revolutionary journal disseminated clandestinely in Russia; played an important role in the development of Social-Democratic thought.

Korolenko, V. G. (1853–1921) writer and journalist.

Kropotkin, P. A. (1842–1921): geographer, historian, great theoretician of anarchism.

Kuusinen, O. (1881–1964): leader of the Finnish communists; active in the Comintern; member of the Central Committee of the C.P.S.U.

Kzhizhanovsky, G. M. (1872–1959): bolshevik since 1903; scientist, member of the Academy of Sciences.

Lepeshinsky, P. N. (1868–1944) and his wife Olga: joined the revolutionary movement in the 1880s; for a time head of the Commissariat of Education in Turkestan; under Stalin was the director of the Museum of the Revolution and of History; Olga Lepeshinskaya was a biologist prominent under Stalin as a member of the Academy of Medical Sciences.

Liquidators: those who after 1907 advocated that the revolutionary activities of the Social-Democrats be abandoned in favour of building up legal workers' organisations.

Lunacharsky, A. V. (1875–1933): People's Commissar of Education from 1917 to 1929; prominent literary critic and author.

Luxemburg, Rosa (1871–1919): one of the greatest Marxist revolutionaries.

Manifesto of 17 October 1905: issued by Tsar Nicholas II under pressure of a general strike, to stave off the revolution; it promised a constitution, civil liberties, etc.; Trotsky exposed the hollowness of the document in one of his most fiery speeches.

Molotov, V. M. (1890–   ): in 1921 one of the secretaries of the Central Committee of the Party; under Stalin a prominent politician and diplomat.

Narodnaya Volya: the illegal organisation of the Narodniks.

Narodniks: Populists; revolutionaries who looked to the peasantry rather than to the workers to take the lead in the overthrowing of tsardom.

Nashe Slovo (Our Word): published by Trotsky in Paris in 1915 with the co-operation of Ryazanov, Lunacharsky, Martov and others.

N.E.P.: New Economic Policy; introduced a measure of private enterprise in trade and small-scale industry.

Olminsky, M. S. (1863–1933): Bolshevik writer; later Chairman of the Institute of Party History.

Ordjonikidze, G.K. (1886–1937): prominent bolshevik; died or committed suicide in the period of Stalin's Purges.

Paris Commune: the proletarian government of Paris; held power from 18 March to 28 May 1871 in the wake of France's defeat in the Franco Prussian war, the main burden of which fell on the working class.

Perovskaya, S. L. (1853–1881): an heroic Russian revolutionary belonging to the Narodniks; sentenced to death and executed for taking part in the attempted assassination of Tsar Alexander II on 1 March 1881.

Pisarev, D. I. (1840–1868): revolutionary writer; spent 4½ years in the Peter and Paul fortress for a clandestine statement in defence of Herzen.

Plekhanov, G. V. (1856–1918): the most eminent exponent of philosophical Marxism.

Pokrovsky, M. N. (1868–1932): Marxist historian.

Populists: see Narodniks.

Rabocheye Delo (The Workers' Cause): published in Geneva between 1899 and 1902; edited by B. N. Krichevsky and A. S. Martynov and giving the Economists' point of view.

Radishchev, A. N. (1749–1802): one of the first representatives of revolutionary Russian thought.

Rech: a daily newspaper of the Constitutional Democrats; appeared from 1906 to 1917.

Red Hill Conspiracy (13 June 1919): was organised by a counter-revolutionary 'national centre' to which belonged several groups, some engaged in spying. The conspirators planned to occupy the fortifications of Kronstadt, to synchronise their action with an offensive on another sector of the front and with an anti-bolshevik rising, and finally to take possession of Petrograd (Leningrad).

Rennenkampf and Meller-Zakomelsky: tsarist generals famous for their brutality after the 1905 revolution.

Rodzianko, M. V. (1859–1924): member of Prince Lvov's government.

Rosta: Russian Press Agency.

Rozengolts, A. P. (1889–1938): member of the Revolutionary War Council headed by Trotsky during the Civil War; perished in Stalin's Purges.

Rykov, A. I. (1881–1938): member of the Politbureau; in 1922 one of Lenin's deputies as Chairman of the Council of the Peoples' Commissars; perished in Stalin's Purges.

Shevchenko, T. G. (1814–1861): Ukrainian poet, writer and painter.

Smena Vekh: a group of anti-bolshevik emigrés who in 1921–2 advocated co-operation with the Soviet government, in the hope that the newly-introduced N.E.P. would lead back towards capitalism.

Social Revolutionaries (S.R.s): a peasant socialist party formed by a merger of several groups among the Narodniks; split into left S.R.s, anarchist in their leanings but participating for a time in Lenin's government, and right S.R.s who supported Kerensky.

Sovremennik (The Contemporary): a literary-political journal, legal but harassed by the authorities; appeared in Petrograd from 1911 to 1915.

Stolypin, P. A. (1862–1911): Prime Minister under Tsar Nicholas II; implemented an agrarian reform designed to put an end to the *mir* and create some well-to-do peasants to stem the revolutionary agitation in the countryside; his name also stands for severe repression after the 1905 revolution.

Thalheimer, A. (1884–1948): one of the founders of the German communist party; later belonged to the anti-Stalinist opposition.

Tsyurupa, A. D. (1870–1928): in 1922 Commissar of Supplies, and one of Lenin's deputies at the Council of the People's Commissars.

Varga, Y. S. (1879–1964): economist of Hungarian origin, Commissar in Bela Kun government and later head of Institute of World Economy in Moscow.

Vekhi (The Landmarks): a symposium of articles by N. Berdyaev, F. Struve and others published in 1909, extremely hostile to the whole revolutionary tradition of Russia.

Vinnichenko, V. K. (1881–1951): Ukrainian novelist; from 1918–1919 Petlura's associate in the anti-bolshevik Ukrainian government.

Vandervelde, E. (1866–1938): leader of the Belgian labour movement; Chairman of the International Bureau of the Second International; member of the government during the First World War.

Zetkin, Klara (1857–1933): German communist since 1919; from 1920 member of the Reichstag.

SOURCES

INTRODUCTION

1. Lenin, *Collected Works*, Vol. 25, p. 492.
2. N. Valentinov, *Encounters with Lenin* (London, O.U.P., 1968), p. 149.
3. H. Marshall (ed.), *Mayakovsky and his poetry* (New York, Pilot Books,), p. 75.
4. *Vospominaniya o Lenine*, Vol. 2 (Moscow, 1957), p. 51.
5. W. Najdus, *Lenin i Krupska w Krakowskim Związku Pomocy dla Więźniów Politycznych* (Cracow, 1965), pp. 86–7.
6. Ya. Makarenko, *Lenin v Polshe* (Moscow, 1957), p. 77.
7. Lenin, op. cit., Vol. 37, pp. 150–1.
8. G. V. Plekhanov, *Literatura i Estetika*, Vol. 2 (Moscow, 1958), p. 175.
9. N. K. Krupskaya, *Lenin o Literature i Iskusstve* (Moscow, 1957), p. 557.
10. A. V. Lunacharsky, *Sobranie Sochinenii*, Vol. 7 (Moscow, 1967), p. 401.
11. *Vospominaniya o Lenine*, Vol. 3 (Moscow, 1960), p. 266.
12. The term was coined by Lunacharsky, op. cit., Vol 1, p. 354.
13. Lenin, op. cit., Vol. 45, p. 374.
14. Lunacharsky, op. cit., Vol. 7, pp. 401–6.
15. *Vospominaniya o Lenine*, Vol. 1 (Moscow, 1956), p. 247.
16. Luncharsky, op. cit., Vol. 3, p. 553.
17. *Vospominaniya o Lenine*, Vol. 1 (Moscow, 1956), pp. 171–2.
18. Lunacharsky, op. cit., Vol. 3, p. 173.
19. Ibid., Vol. 7, p. 405.
20. F. Engels to J. Bloch, 21 September 1890, in *Marx and Engels, Selected Correspondence* (London, 1943), p. 476.
21. Note of Lenin's secretary of 14 February 1923 in *Collected Works*, Vol. 42, p. 493.
22. Lenin, op. cit., Vol. 33, p. 306.
23. Ibid., Vol. 33, p. 288.
24. Ibid., Vol. 33, p. 257.
25. Ibid., Vol. 36, p. 593, here translated from *Sochineniya*, Vol. 45, p. 343.
26. Lenin, op. cit., Vol 33, p. 315.
27. Ibid., Vol. 36, pp. 593–7.

I. WORK AND LEISURE

1. G. M. Kzhizhanovsky, *Velikii Lenin* (Moscow, 1956), pp. 18–20, 4–5, 34–5.

2. (i) O. P. Lepeshinskaya, 'Vstrechi s Ilyichem' (Moscow, 1957), pp. 8–9 and (ii) P. N. Lepeshinsky, 'Around Lenin', both in G. V. Bulatsky, *Oruzhem Slova* (Moscow, 1968), p. 94.
3. P. N. Lepeshinsky, *Na Povorote* (Moscow, 1955), pp. 94–5, 109–10.
4. Ibid., pp. 108–9.
5. T. S. Bobrovskaya (Zelikson), 'Stranitsy iz revolutsionnovo Proshlovo', in *Vospominaniya o Lenine* (Moscow, 1956), Vol. 1, pp. 240–1.
6. M. Essen, 'Vstrechi s Leninym', in *Vospominaniya*, Vol. 1, pp. 247, 251–4.
7. S. J. Bagotsky, 'V. I. Lenin v Krakove i Poronine', in *Vospominaniya*, Vol. 1, pp. 437–56.

II. LIKE ANY OTHER MAN?

1. M. N. Pokrovsky, *Oktyabrskaya Revolutsiya* (Moscow, 1929), pp. 13–17, 94.
2. V. D. Bonch-Bruevich, *Izbrannye Sochineniya* (Moscow, 1963), Vol. 3, pp. 399–405.
3. Ibid., pp. 406–11.
4. Lenin, *Collected Works*, Vol. 35, p. 112.
5. Bonch-Bruevich, op. cit., pp. 28–9.
6. Ibid., pp. 296–7.
7. S. K. Gil, *Vospominaniya o Lenine* (Moscow, 1957), Vol. 2, pp. 435–7.
8. Lenin, op. cit., Vol. 35, p. 333.
9. Ibid., Vol. 45, p. 556.
10. Ibid., Vol. 44, p. 327.
11. Ibid., Vol. 45, pp. 407–8.
12. Ibid., Vol. 45, p. 504.
13. Ibid., Vol. 35, p. 454.
14. Ibid., Vol. 44, p. 371.
15. Lenin, *Sochineniya*, Russian edn., Vol. 52, p. 276.

III. INESSA ARMAND

1. Lenin, *Collected Works*, Vol. 43, p. 400.
2. Ibid., Vol. 35, pp. 144–5.
3. Ibid., Vol. 43, pp. 409–10.
4. Ibid., Vol. 43, pp. 417–20.
5. Ibid., Vol. 43, p. 432.
6. Ibid., Vol. 43, p. 424.
7. Ibid., Vol. 43, pp. 454–5.
8. Translated from Lenin, *Sochineniya*, 5th Russian edn., Vol. 49, pp. 78–80.
9. Ibid., Vol. 49, p. 173.
10. Lenin, *Collected Works*, Vol. 43, pp. 504–5.

11. Ibid., Vol. 43, pp. 505–6.
12. Ibid., Vol. 43, p. 507.
13. Ibid., Vol. 35, pp. 246–7.
14. Ibid., Vol. 35, pp. 248–9.
15. Ibid., Vol. 35, pp. 250–1.
16. Ibid., Vol. 35, pp. 260–1.
17. Ibid., Vol. 35, p. 264.
18. Ibid., Vol. 35, pp. 268–9.
19. Ibid., Vol. 35, p. 598–9.
20. Ibid., Vol. 43, p. 599.
21. Ibid., Vol. 43, p. 602.
22. Ibid., Vol. 43, p. 603.
23. Ibid., Vol. 35, p. 272.
24. Ibid., Vol. 35, pp. 306–7.
25. P Podlyashchuk, *Tovarishch Inessa* (Moscow, 1963).
26. Angelica Balabanoff, *Impressions of Lenin*, pp. 14–15.
27. Marcel Body, 'Alexandra Kollontay', in *Preuves* (April 1952).

IV. REVOLUTION, LITERATURE AND ART

1. Lenin, *Collected Works*, Vol. 5, pp. 509–10.
2. N. Valentinov, *Encounters with Lenin* (London, O.U.P., 1968), trans. by Paul Rosta and Brian Pearce, pp. 105–7.
3. Ibid., Vol. 18, pp. 25–31.
4. Ibid., Vol. 15, pp. 202–9.
5. Ibid., Vol. 16, pp. 330–2.
6. Ibid., Vol. 16, pp. 353–4.
7. Ibid., Vol. 17, pp. 49–53.
8. Ibid., Vol. 13, pp. 475–8.
9. Ibid., Vol. 17, pp. 139–43.
10. Lenin, *Sochineniya*, Russian edn, Vol. 12, pp. 99–105.
11. Lenin, *Collected Works*, Vol. 19, pp. 277–9.
12. Ibid., Vol. 33, pp. 462–4.
13. Klara Zetkin, *Reminiscences of Lenin* (London, 1929).
14. Lenin, *Collected Works*, Vol. 35, pp. 121–4.
15. Ibid., Vol. 35, pp. 410–14.
16. Translated from Lenin, *Sochineniya*, 5th Russian edn, Vol. 51, pp. 47–9.
17. Lenin, *Collected Works*, Vol. 35, p. 415.
18. A. V. Lunacharsky, *Sobranie Sochinenii*, Vol. 4, p. 438.
19. Translated from Lenin, *Sochineniya*, 5th Russian edn, Vol. 54, pp. 265–6. See also *Collected Works*, Vol. 45, pp. 555–6.
20. A. V. Lunacharsky, 'Lenin i iskusstvo', in *Collected Works* (Moscow, 1967), Vol. 7, pp. 401–7.
21. Lenin, *Collected Works*, Vol. 45, pp. 138–9.
22. Translated from Lenin, *Sochineniya*, 5th Russian edn, Vol. 52, p. 180. See also *Collected Works*, Vol. 45, p. 139.

23. Lenin, *Collected Works*, Vol. 33, pp. 223–4.
24. I. A. Armand, 'Poezdka vo Vkhutemas', in *Vospominaniya*, Vol. 3, pp. 327–30.
25. S. Senkin, quoted in E. Dobin, *Lenin i Iskusstvo*, p. 225.
26. M. Garlovsky, quoted in ibid., pp. 225–6.
27. M. Garlovsky, quoted in ibid., p. 138.
28. N. Altman, quoted in ibid., pp. 226–7.
29. Y. Yakovlev, quoted in ibid., p. 229.
30. A. V. Lunacharsky, quoted in ibid., p. 172.
31. G. M. Kzhizhanovsky, *Velikii Lenin* (Moscow, 1956), pp. 22–4.
32. V. D. Bonch-Bruevich, quoted in op. cit., pp. 76–7.
33. A. V. Lunacharsky, *Literaturnaya Gazeta* 4–5 (29 January 1933).
34. Lenin, *Collected Works*, Vol. 35, p. 360.
35. Quoted from *Samoye Vazhnoye iz Vsekh Iskusstv* (Moscow, 1963).
36. Lenin, *Collected Works*, Vol. 42, pp. 388–9.
37. A. V. Lunacharsky, *Sobranie Sochinenii*, Vol. 7, p. 404.
38. M. Stetskevich, quoted in Dobin, op. cit., pp. 192–3.

V. WOMEN'S RIGHTS

1. Lenin, *Collected Works*, Vol. 35, pp. 180–1.
2. Ibid., Vol. 35, pp. 182–5.
3. Ibid., Vol. 29, pp. 428–9.
4. Ibid., Vol. 30, pp. 40–6.
5. Ibid., Vol. 30, 120–2.
6. Klara Zetkin, *Reminiscences of Lenin* (London, 1929).

VI. BUREAUCRACY

1. V. D. Bonch-Bruevich, *Izbrannye Sochineniya* (Moscow, 1963), pp. 166–72.
2. Lenin, *Collected Works*, Vol. 32, p. 48.
3. Ibid., Vol. 33, pp. 224–5.
4. Ibid., Vol. 33, pp. 256–7.
5. This passage is translated from the 5th Russian edition of Lenin's *Sochineniya*, Vol. 45, p. 88; in *Collected Works*, Vol. 33, p. 279.
6. Lenin, *Collected Works*, Vol. 33, pp. 289–309.
7. The text of this note is translated from the 5th Russian edition of Lenin's *Sochineniya*, Vol. 45, p. 214; the text in Vol. 33, p. 372 of the English edition is slightly different and the name of L. B. Kamenev has been omitted.
8. Lenin, *Collected Works*, Vol. 33, p. 444.
9. Translated from the 5th Russian edition of Lenin's *Sochineniya*, Vol. 45, pp. 356–60; see also *Collected Works*, Vol. 36, pp. 605–9.

INDEX

256 *Index*